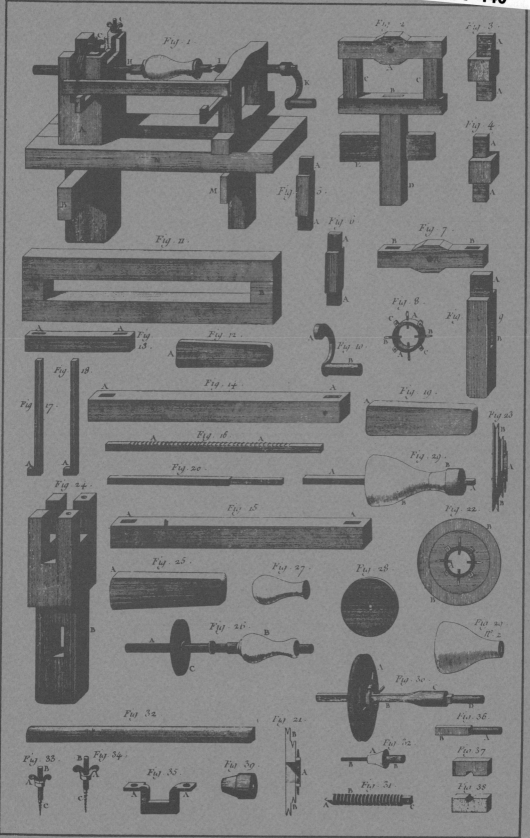

Potier d'Etain, Tour.

The American Pewterer

The research for this publication was partially supported by
a grant from the Penrose Fund of the American Philo-
sophical Society

The American Pewterer

His Techniques & His Products

Henry J. Kauffman

Professor, Industrial Arts Education
Millersville State College
Millersville, Pa.

Drawings by
Dorothy Briggs
Staff Artist
Smithsonian Institution
Washington, D.C.

Thomas Nelson

Library of Congress Catalog Card Number: 77-113170

Printed in the United States of America

Acknowledgments

Writing this part of a book is doubtless the most pleasant part of the total work. Pleasant, not only because it is evidence that long hours of research and writing have been completed, but also because it gives the author an opportunity to thank the various people and organizations for the invaluable help they have given in assembling the contents of the book.

Work that has been done over a long period of time does not permit the author to keep a perfect record of all who made contributions to the survey. To the unnamed contributors I am grateful, and ask their pardon in not recording their names. I do want to especially thank Charles Hummel and John J. Evans of the Henry Francis du Pont Winterthur Museum for their generous contributions and advice. I would also like to thank Mr. Ledlie Laughlin, the author of *Pewter in America*, for allowing me to use the enumeration of tools and for other help over the years. I am also indebted to the photographic and public relations departments of The Brooklyn Museum, the Henry Francis du Pont Winterthur Museum, The Metropolitan Museum of Art, the Philadelphia Museum of Art, and the Smithsonian Institution for the photographs and data they supplied which aid materially in making this a constructive and attractive book.

I am also grateful to the Metropolitan Museum of Art for permission to reprint *American Pewterers and Their Marks,* an important contribution to this study.

Finally, I would like to emphasize that the unique part of this book is the attractive drawings made by Dorothy Briggs. Her knowledge of technical drawing, her aesthetic sensitivity, and her tireless patience in dealing with the minutia of the drawings are fully appreciated by the author.

The inevitable errors which appear in a survey of this type are the responsibility of the author who will be grateful for corrections and constructive criticisms.

Contents

The American Pewterer

Introduction

It is quite apparent that the collecting *cognescenti* of pewter objects recognize in them an indefinable "mystique." There is about them an aura which no other objects of metal possess, a glamor which is very difficult, if not impossible, for anyone "on the outside" to understand or define.

As with most intangibles, this condition does not fit a formula for scientific analysis. For example, although the metal inherently has little value, today a good tankard is worth five thousand dollars. Pewter is composed largely of tin, which is considered to be inexpensive—and it is when compared with silver and gold, but not in relation to iron. The "image" of tin has suffered unjustifiably because the early Fords were called "tin lizzies" and in modern times a discarded tin can is regarded as completely worthless.

It might also be pointed out that because of the mode of production there are few pieces among the total quantity available to collectors which can be classified as unique. There is an inkstand and an oval platter by Henry Will, a globular teapot by Love, and a few rare coffeepots by William Will, but, by and large, the market place offers objects made by reasonably prolific makers such as the Boardmans and other craftsmen of the eighteenth and nineteenth centuries. Some of these objects have subtle differences which only experts can detect; many of these continue to rest in the cupboards and attics of the owners, who are not aware of the importance of their possessions.

The color of the metal has given it a bad reputation, and one dealer

Table set with objects made of pewter. Although the objects differ in style and period, there is a certain compatibility which results in a pleasing variety. *Kauffman collection*

11

known to the writer made a specialty of canvasing the countryside inquiring if anyone had any dull "lead plates."

Years of neglect and disuse have allowed the formulation of an oxide on pewter which is both unsightly and difficult to remove. Often this oxide has eaten holes through the metal, which become evident only after the deposit is removed and the bare metal exposed. Most people shudder when they are told that a mild solution of lye and water will remove the oxide without harming the metal; for this and other reasons many pieces continue to deteriorate when they should be saved from eventual destruction.

Possibly the most unfavorable criticism of pewter objects is the fact that they were essentially the products of a machine. Most of the molds were made on a lathe, and the products were skimmed and burnished on a lathe, with only a minimum of handwork in joining the parts and finishing the objects. In the nineteenth century, the stamping and spinning techniques became so popular that many duplicates were made, all virtually identical, but in some cases reasonably attractive and eagerly sought by the collecting fraternity today.

After the first quarter of the nineteenth century many changes occurred in the business of pewter making. Expensive molds were discarded for inexpensive forms (chucks) over which thin sheets of britannia metal were shaped. This metal had no lead and consisted entirely of tin, copper, and antimony. The fact that it had been rolled into sheets caused it to be more compact, it was tougher than the earlier alloy, and it was polished to a luster comparable to that of silver.

In the past, much attention has been given to such facets of collecting as the names of makers, the regions where they worked, and the relative value of different pieces. As a matter of fact, one book concerned mostly with values has become a rare commodity on the book market today. The contemporary age of technology has brought another dimension to the collecting of pewter, and this is the primary function of this survey. This added knowledge will help to create a new generation of discriminating buyers who will have the most complete comprehension of their medium that has ever been available. It is likely that the crescendo of seeking will increase, but unfortunately the supply is rapidly diminishing.

Pewter

THE METAL

BEFORE surveying the methods used to make objects of pewter in the eighteenth century in America, it is well to know something about the metals then in use. Seventeenth-century products need not be considered, for the metal and methods of the eighteenth century were used in the earlier period, and the number of surviving pieces is negligible. Indeed, a pewter spoon made by John Copeland at Chuckatuck, Virginia, and possibly some plates by Dolbeare are the only known pieces of seventeenth-century American pewter extant.

S. E. HAMLIN,

PEWTERER and BRAZIER,

Nearly oppofite the Epifcopal Church,

RESPECTFULLY informs the public, that he continues his bufinefs at the old ftand, where he offers at whole-fale and retail, a handfome affortment of

Pewter-Ware,

of a quality and price as to render unnecef-fary the importation of foreign ware.

ALSO,

Block-Tin and other Tea-Pots
Ditto Tumblers and Soup Ladles
Tutania Table and Tea Spoons
Iron   do.   do.
Lead Weights of every fize in ufe
Deep Sea and Hand Leads
Window do.
And fundry articles of Brafs Ware.

LIKEWISE FOR SALE,

A fecond-hand Wheel with Frame and Crank, fuitable for a Block-Maker or Founder.

Orders from the neighboring towns or country faithfully attended to.

☞ Cafh paid for old Pewter, Brafs and Copper.

June 24.

Advertisement of Samuel Hamlin in the *Providence* [R.I.] *Gazette,* Oct. 9, 1809. The craftsman's need for old metal is very apparent in this advertisement. *Kauffman collection*

13

Generally speaking, various tin-based metals were used for making the so-called "pewter-ware," which included both the pewter of the eighteenth century and the britannia metal of the nineteenth. Not only were the metals of these two centuries dissimilar, but the objects were fabricated differently. For the record, it can be stated simply that objects made of pewter were cast while those made of britannia were stamped or spun, this being one of the ways by which the products of the two centuries can be distinguished.

Let us first consider pewter and the molds used to cast it. To inquire into the nature of American pewter, one must of necessity look into the contents of English pewter. Because there were no tin mines in America and the mercantile plans of England did not permit the exportation of unwrought pewter, the American craftsman was almost wholly dependent for his metal on damaged or discarded pieces of European pewter, most of which came from England.

Scrutiny of the Public (shipping) Records of England in the eighteenth century indicates that only finished pieces of pewter were shipped to America. R. W. Symonds reporting in *Antiques* (October, 1935) on the quantity exported to America, Georgia excluded, between 1697 and 1767, noted that even before 1700 yearly shipments of pewter were valued at more than £4,000; by 1760, at more than £38,000. Ledlie Laughlin, in *Pewter in America,* points out that the yearly value of such large shipments ran in excess of a million dollars in today's currency. Even more startling is his observation that the value of the pewter shipments exceeded the combined value of imported furniture, silverplate, and tinware.

Because it was from these finished English pieces, melted down and reworked, that most American pewter was fashioned, it behooves us to briefly review the production of pewter objects in England. There, by the 1700s, standard practices were in effect concerning all aspects of pewter production. These rules were enforced by the guilds, each major city having a guild, whose officers were charged with the task of assaying the alloys used by member craftsmen.

The alloys used at mid-century are reported by E. Chambers in his *Cyclopedia of Arts and Sciences* (London, 1752):

> Pewter, a factitious metal, used in domestic utensils. Its basis is tin, which
> is converted into pewter by the mixture of six pounds of brass, and fifteen

pounds of lead to a hundred-weight of tin. Beside this composition, which makes common pewter, there are others for other occasions, compounded of tin, mixed with regulus of antimony, bismuth, and copper in several proportions.

The variety of alloys is further suggested by Edward J. Gale, in *Pewter and the Amateur Collector,*

> There are something like forty authentic variations [of pewter] recorded, and in reality the composition as actually put forth by makers of different times and countries was, if of a certain similarity, constantly so variable as to place the whole matter in its intricacies beyond the collector's interest, and wholly in the hands of the analytic chemist. . . .
>
> It is generally assumed that from the first quality were made plates and platters, etc.; from the second, standing vessels, bowls, etc.; and from alloys having a greater percentage of lead, cheaper vessels for public-house use.

Using the alloys of English pewter for production in America does not imply that all American pewter was the same quality as that from which it was derived. There was considerable variation. One American maker is known for the poor quality of the metal he used; others might have tried to upgrade the metal brought to them for casting important objects, such as tankards, communion flagons, and christening bowls; and an itinerant pewterer might have snipped a small piece of pewter from each vessel he received to recast, thereby accumulating enough metal for a new vessel which he could sell on his route over the countryside. The profit from such a piece would be high, for it cost only the lead which had been substituted for the stolen pewter.

In England, where guilds imposed penalties on pewterers who did not use the alloys prescribed, a certain amount of control over the alloy was achieved. A craftsman's first infraction was followed by a warning not to repeat the offense; his second, by confiscation of all his objects he made of substandard metal; his third, by exclusion from the guild. The repeating offender, thus punished, frequently retreated to a rural, uncontrolled area, where he continued to make substandard pewterware. For obvious reasons, he usually neglected to identify his product with his mark.

No doubt some of this substandard ware was shipped to America where there were no guilds to assay products, and a craftsman could follow any procedure he wished in regard to the quality of the metal.

Despite this possibility, and even though standard metal was cast and recast a number of times in America, the quality of the metal remained reasonably high. If the American craftsman faltered at all, it was in his workmanship rather than in the quality of the alloy he used.

A matter of concern to the collector is the ratio of tin (usually about 90 per cent) to the amounts of copper, lead, bismuth, brass, or antimony used in the making of a vessel. If he is concerned mostly with esthetics, he will find heavily leaded pewter less attractive than better grades; if he is a practical collector, and wishes to use his collection, he may consider heavily leaded pieces dangerous for serving food or brewing tea.

There are a number of ways to determine the content of the alloy. One simple test, other than woman's intuition, is to snap the edge of a piece with finger or pencil to hear it "ring." Pewter with 20 per cent lead produces a dull sound; that in which virtually no lead is present is very resonant. A dull gray appearance is another evidence of high lead content. A test, impractical except for plates and other flatware, is to bend the piece slightly. Because tin makes a cracking sound when it is bent, pewter with a high tin content will do the same. However, these are unscientific tests. The only precise way to determine the content of the alloy is to have a metallurgical analysis made.

Collectors need have some concern as to the melting point of alloys. If they put a vessel on a hot stove, they will discover the melting point is relatively low! Most of the alloys melt in a range of 400 to 500 degrees Fahrenheit. For casting, the metal was heated in an iron kettle or ladle over a forge fire. The container held more metal than was needed for one casting, so that a completely new batch did not have to be melted for each successive casting. Within a few minutes after pouring, the metal became solid and the vessel could be removed before the mold was completely cooled. After the cast vessel was removed, another pouring of molten metal formed another object, this procedure continuing until all the desired objects were produced.

THE WORKSHOP

Despite the wide range of interest among collectors, historians, technologists, museum personnel, and antique dealers, the procedures followed in making objects of pewter in the eighteenth century are virtually unknown today. As a matter of fact, the lack of technological information about the two trades (silversmithing and pewtering), combined with the fact that their products are very similar in design, has led many to believe that in the eighteenth century a craftsman worked in both media. The writer has not found one example of such a practice; however, it cannot be said positively that no craftsman worked at one time or another in both metals.

The reason for such a precise division between the two trades lies simply in the fact that the metals, being vastly dissimilar in physical qualities, were formed by different methods. It must be pointed out that the basic tools of the silversmith were the hammer, anvil, punch, and vise. Virtually all major vessels were formed with a hammer, while appendages, such as knobs, finials, and handles, were cast. There is not only historical evidence to substantiate this opinion; close examination of the objects (especially of the interior) supports this hypothesis.

The major equipment of the pewterer, as revealed by studies of inventories, examinations of pewter objects, and referrals to encyclopedias of the eighteenth century, consisted of many molds of either brass or bronze. Simple pieces, such as plates and spoons, were cast in one mold, consisting of two parts, while objects such as tankards and teapots required a mold for each of the various parts, which were then joined and finished on a lathe. The inventory of Thomas Byles shows that the total weight of his molds was 1,183 pounds.

Generally speaking, the admirers of American silver are better informed about the mode of manufacture of objects of silver than are those of their associates who are interested in pewter. This condition exists because a sizeable number of books on the subject of antique silver contain pertinent information about fabrication, while *Pewter in America,* by Ledlie Laughlin, is the only book about American pewter which furnishes any insights into the methods by which objects were produced. Unfortunately, this fine book was rather expensive when it appeared in 1940 and has been out of print for many years.

It should also be pointed out that a number of silver craftsmen working in America continue to work in the old traditions of their trade, which is not true of those working in pewter. As a matter of fact, some producers of pewter objects imply that they are using the procedures of the eighteenth century, but close examination of their facilities re-

Pewter and Pewter Equipment Listed in the Inventory of Thomas Byles

Presented September 10, 1771, at Philadelphia by Benjamin Harbeson, Jr. and William Will

Old pewter	10 lbs.	at 10d	0. 8.4
Do	2328 do	" 9d	87. 6.0
Pewr Ware rough Cast	687 "	" 13d	37. 4.3
Pewter plates	567 "	" 18d	42.10.6
Do basons	610 "	" 18d	45.15.0
Wrought dishes	419 "	" 20d	34.18.4
do basons	318 "	" 20½d	27. 3.3
do plates	792 "	" 19d	62.14.0
Hd plates	68 "	" 2s	6.16.0
19 Watter plates		8d	7.12.0
1 Gall Wine Measure			0.15.0
3 ½ Gal do do		10	1.10.0
19 Qt do do		6	5.14.0
30 Pt. do do		3/6	5. 5.0
39 ½ Pt. do do		2	3.18.0
24 Gill do do		20d	2. 0.0
87 Quart Potts		3.6	15. 4.6
12 Pint Potts		2	1. 4.0
63 Quart Hd Mugs		4	12.12.0
13 Quart Hd do		5	3. 5.0
25 Hd Pint do		3	3.15.0
31 Common Qt Bellied mugs		3.6	5. 8.6
38 Qt Hd Tankards		5.6	10. 9.0
28 Qt Common do		5	7. 0.0
58 Strait Bodied do		5	14.10.0
5 Bellied Pt do		3	0.15.0
3 Pt Hd do		3/6	0.10.6
89 Quart Hd Bowles		2s.	8.18.0
82 Pint do		18d.	6. 3.0
55 Lg. Close stool pans		10	27.10.0
3 Sm. do do do		7	1. 1.0
7 Lg. Bed pans		15	5. 5.0
4 Sm. do do		12	2. 8.0
18 Chamr potts		5	4.10.0
20 Hd do do		6	6. 0.0
42 doz 6 Porringers			30.10.0
28 doz Hd do		24s per doz.	33.12.0
37 Tea Potts			8.14.0
4 2 Qt Coffee Potts		18	3.12.0
8 3 Pt do do		15	6. 0.0
9 Qt do do		10	4.10.0
3 Pt do do		6	0.18.0
44 Sugar Basons with Covers		2s	4. 8.0
24 Qt Black Jacks		2/6	3. 0.0
24 ½ Pt. Cup with handles		1s	1. 4.0
15 ½ Pt. Cups no handles		10d	0.12.6
14 Sm. Pewr Cups		9d	0.10.6
48 Pt. Dram Bottles		2s	4.16.0
7 ½ Pt. do do		20d	0.11.8
15 Sucking do		3/6	2.12.6
6 Challices pewr		6	1.16.0
23 Soop spoons		2	2. 6.0
43 Hd Table do			0.17.6
36 doz. Com. do do		3/6	6. 6.0
46 doz Tea spoons			2. 6.0
1 Cullinder			0.12.0

2 Cullinders			1.10.0
86 Pewr Salts		10d	3.11.8
1 Plate Cover & funnel			0. 6.6
7 doz 8 Candlesticks		7	2.13.8
8 Bottle cranes		3.6	2. 8.0
39 pr Cotton & wool cards		3	5. 8.0
9 pr. flasks & screws			0.12.0
12 Barbers basons		5	3. 0.0
3 do Potts		5	0.15.0
1 Oval Standish			1. 2.6
9 Lg. Chest Standishes			5. 8.0
2 Lead Inkstands			0. 5.0
Pewter curtain rings	14 lbs		1. 1.0
Brass molds	1183	2/6	147.17.6
Pewter do	188	13d	10. 3.8
Brasier stakes &	lbs. oz.		
Beak Irons	454.12	9d	17. 0.9
1 Pewterers anvil	29		1. 9.0
9 Brasiers heads	44.8		2. 4.6
2 Vices	56	4d	0.18.8
130 files		6d	3. 6.0
1 Pr. Shears			1. 1.0
1 Sm. Anvil	31	4d	0.10.4
28 Hammers		6d	0.14.0
12 Pewterers do		2/6	1.10.0
1 Upright Drill			0. 5.0
1 Solder Mortar & pestle			0. 2.6
Punches, Chisels &c.		66 at 2d	0.11.0
30 New Hooks		18d	2. 5.0
27 Hooks Usefull			1. 7.0
32 Hook shanks		1½d	0. 4.0
5 Wheel burnishers			0. 7.6
Old Iron	500 lbs.	1½d	3. 2.6
101 Sundry Iron tools		4d	1.13.8
1 Cast Iron Stand			0.10.0
2 pr Shears 2 pr Pinchers			0. 9.9
24 Molds and Paterns		13d	1. 6.0
50 Blocks with Burnings			2.10.0
8 Spoon Bows &c.		18d	0.12.0
10 Graters & Burnishers		4d	0. 3.4
2 Pr Lg. Bellows			2. 0.0
1 Old Brass Ketle			0. 5.0
Cast Iron Weights			0. 7.6
1 Pewterers Wheel &c			2.10.0
1 Pewterers Anvill & Spoon test	321 lbs.	15d	2. 0.0
Sundry files, floats, Ladles &c			0. 9.6
1 Small Anvill	10 lbs.	6d	0. 5.0
2 Screw plates & taps			0. 5.0
Old Lead Weights	34 lbs.	3d	0. 8.6
Brass do	14 lbs.		1. 8.0
12 Scale Beams &c.			4. 0.0
46 Nest Crucibles			2. 6.0
15 Black Lead do			2. 4.0
Rotten stone &c.	22 lbs.		1. 2.0
60 Bushel Coal			1.10.0
Tin glass & Bismuth	10.4	2/6	1. 5.7

Total Inventory £1517. 18.5

Inventory of tools and objects of Thomas Byles, a famous craftsman working in Philadelphia, Pennsylvania, in the eighteenth century. William Will and Benjamin Harbeson
were both pewterers. Harbeson, however, achieved his fame as an outstanding copper-
smith of the era. From *Pewter in America* by Ledlie Laughlin. *Courtesy of the author*

veals that they are not. In the 1920s a large producer made many objects of pewter in the style of the eighteenth century, but the method of fabrication was not of the period.

The void of knowledge about methods used to fabricate objects of pewter exists also because scarcely any of the major tools (the molds) of the pewterer have survived, and virtually none have been reproduced. Although a reasonably large number of molds for casting pewter spoons can be found throughout the country, and a few molds for making buttons, less than a dozen large molds for making plates, basins, teapots, and the like, are known. A scattering of tools used by Samuel Pierce can be seen in Old Deerfield, Massachusetts, and a number of molds for casting plates and basins are on display at Old Salem, in Winston-Salem, North Carolina, but no original or restored shop *per se* can be seen in America.

There are, however, some European sources available, showing the facilities of the pewterer of the eighteenth century. Insofar as most of the early American craftsmen were trained in Europe, most researchers conclude that the facilities here were similar to those of Europe. At least, the workmanship on such objects as silverware, guns, ships, and so forth, gives evidence of a similarity in methods of construction.

It is believed that the workshops generally consisted of one big room where all activity from designing to selling was transacted. Possibly, there was at least one division separating the production from the display and sales areas. An illustration in a Dutch publication of the late seventeenth century shows a sales room with an entry from the street. Within the room are shelves loaded with finished pieces of pewter on display, in front of which is a counter with a sales person holding a number of very large plates. This person almost certainly could have been the master craftsman. Before the counter a young man is carrying a pile of pewter plates, which are presumably finished and ready for delivery to a customer. This boy could well have been an apprentice. The workshop facilities were probably located behind the shelves, out of sight as far as the average customer was concerned.

The *Diderot Encyclopedia* of the eighteenth century shows a typical French pewterer's shop, which was presumably located to the rear of a sales room, since no sales or exhibition area is shown. Within the shop is

Sales room of a Dutch pewterer in the late seventeenth century. Some of the objects are typical Dutch forms. From *Het Menschelyke Bedryf* by Jan Luyken, Amsterdam, 1694. *Courtesy Eric de Jonge*

Workshop of a French pewterer, illustrated in the *Diderot Encyclopedia*. *Courtesy Smithsonian Institution*

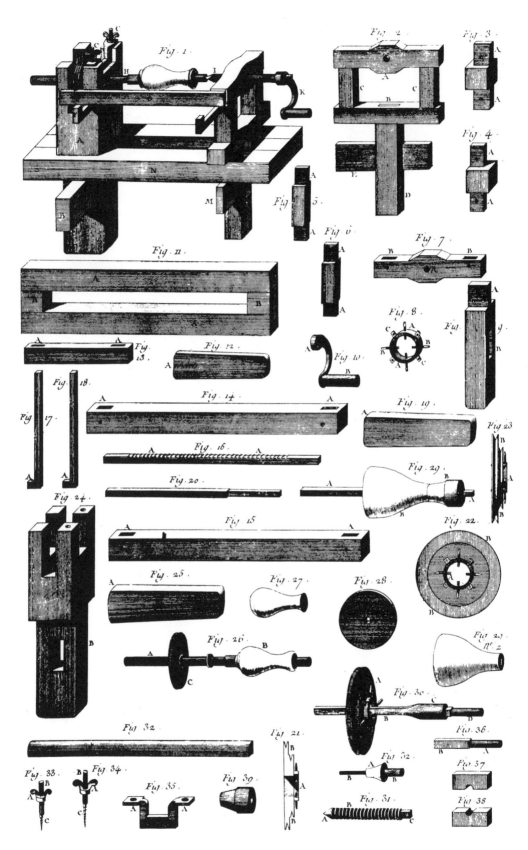

Potier d'Etain, Tour

a large forge with a hood to catch the smoke and direct it into the chimney. Nearby is a table with a closed mold for making plates resting on it. A craftsman is pouring molten metal into the mold. Along the wall with windows a lathe is located, powered by a large wheel and a belt which was turned by an apprentice or a laborer. A craftsman working at the lathe is shaping an object of pewter between centers; however, the position of the turner does not permit the form of the vessel to be identified.

From other illustrations in that encyclopedia it is evident that two types of lathes were used by the pewterer, both constructed largely of wood. One was equipped to turn objects between centers as is done today on a modern lathe for turning metal or wood. The other has a headstock facility to which plates and other hollow ware were attached to skim the surface and make it smooth. The ridges found on the bottom of plates and porringers are evidences of the workman's using this type of lathe with a skimming tool.

A set of cutting tools for use on the lathe is also illustrated. The objects were fastened into either type of lathe, and the tool was supported on a horizontal bar, brought as near as possible to the object being turned to reduce vibration of the tool and the object. Tools in a great variety of shapes were required for such work, and they had to be kept unusually sharp to function satisfactorily.

Although the location and function of these various facilities of the workshop are helpful and interesting, of more importance is the designing and making of the molds which were used to create all the forms of pewter in the eighteenth century. Surprisingly little comment on the subject of molds has been made in American and European books about pewter. Perhaps because so few molds have survived, interest in pewter turned first in other directions—to makers, locations, styles, values, and so on. Today, with so much research already accomplished in these areas, technologically minded collectors are expressing great interest in the "how."

Most eighteenth-century molds were made of either brass or bronze. In the nineteenth century, some were constructed of cast iron. These

Lathe for skimming objects of pewter between centers (Fig. 1). The rest of the figures show details of its disassembled parts. From *Diderot Encyclopedia. Courtesy Smithsonian Institution*

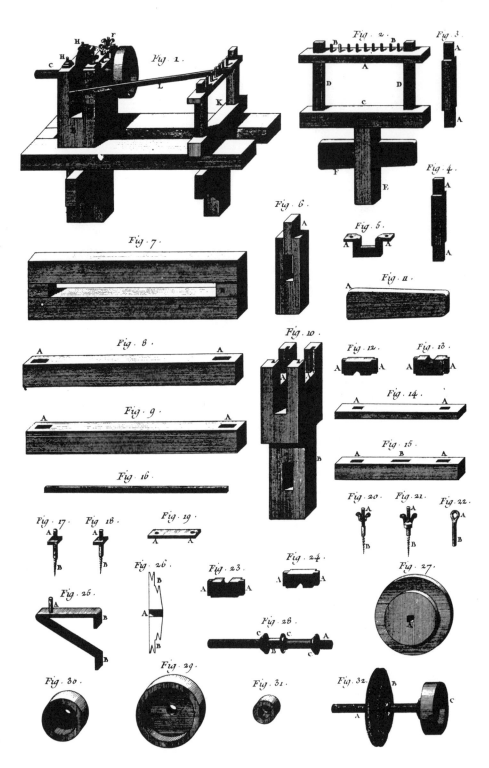

Potier d'Etain, Tour

Lathe with a headstock facility for skimming flat objects, principally plates and basins (Fig. 1). The rest of the figures show the various parts in detail. Most of the parts were made of wood. From *Diderot Encyclopedia. Courtesy Smithsonian Institution*

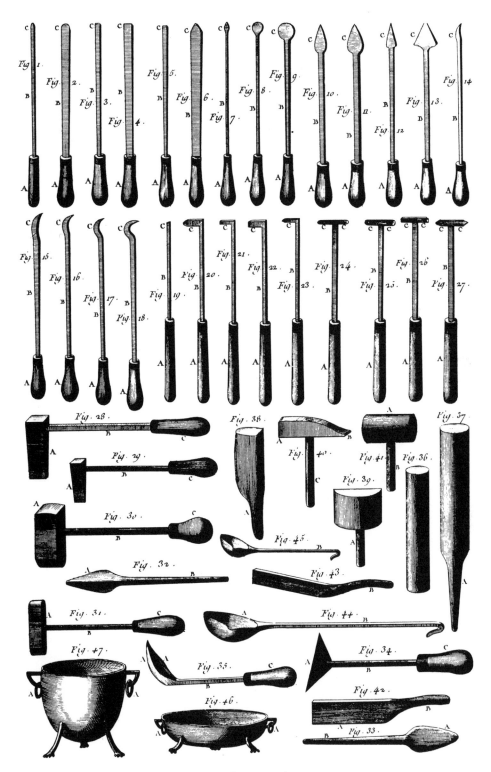

Potier d'Etain, outils.

Skimming tools, soldering irons, ladles, mallets, etc., used by the pewterer in fabricating his ware. From *Diderot Encyclopedia. Courtesy Smithsonian Institution*

metals were used because they could be heated many times without appreciable deterioration. They also retained heat over a long period of time, which made them very practicable for the work they were designed to do.

Doubtless the most elusive answer in the whole technology of making vessels of pewter is: Who designed these molds? The answer is particularly important, for the mold was not only the means to the production of pewter vessels, but was also the factor which determined the design of the vessel. Unlike the silversmith, who could create a different design every time he made a tankard, the pewterer was bound to his pattern, its height and diameter, with only a little freedom in varying the moldings on the edges or eliminating them completely, if he cared to.

Objects cast of brass or bronze today are made from patterns executed by a trade of craftsmen called "pattern-makers." There is no evidence that such a trade existed in the eighteenth century. None of the earliest directories of New York, Boston, or Philadelphia list such tradesmen, and very few appear before the middle of the nineteenth century. For the moment, the question of who made the patterns for the molds must remain unanswered.

There is also the problem of where the molds were made. Because of the advanced technological knowledge and experience needed to produce them, one might logically look toward Europe for the solution; however, there is evidence that some molds were made here. Although few, if any, spoon molds have been identified as products of American craftsmen, the fact that great numbers have been found here, while they are relatively scarce in Europe, suggests that some must have been made in America. As a matter of fact, there is documentary proof that they were made here. A newspaper advertisement, published in the *Pennsylvania Gazette* for May 3, 1752, clearly announces this actuality:

THOMAS GREGORY

In Third Street, Philadelphia, opposite Church Alley and near Market Street, makes and sells all sorts of brass work suitable for mills, heads for dogs [andirons], brass dogs, shovels and tongs, candlesticks of all sorts, *spoon molds,* shoe buckles, bell metal skillets, kettles, house and horse bells, and a variety of other things too tedious to mention, at the most reasonable rates.

N.B. The said Gregory turns all sorts of iron, brass, pewter, and silver, likewise gives the best price for old brass, and mends all sorts of brass work.

The manufacturing of these molds was not an easy task; certainly it was a tedious one. First, the pattern of a proposed mold had to be made of wood. This pattern was then placed in damp sand to make an exact cavity of the pattern. When the pattern was removed, molten brass or bronze was poured into the empty recess remaining in the sand. After it had cooled, the intended inner portion of the cast mold had to be shaped and made smooth. If the mold was to be round, the inner portion was finished on a lathe. If it were not round, it had to be laboriously scraped and abraded by hand methods. A great deal of time went into making the mold as perfect as possible, for it was more economical to spend time with the mold and have perfect castings than to file and polish irregularities on every piece cast in an imperfect mold.

Although small spoon and button molds show evidence of considerable skill and craftsmanship in their finish, it is the big plate molds that excite the imagination of today's technologist. It seems incredible that molds for plates, sometimes weighing as much as fifty pounds, could be so meticulously finished on the lathes of that time. Much of the lathe itself was made of wood and the power source was a treadle or a wheel operated by an apprentice or other unskilled craftsman. A fit of watertight accuracy was required where the various pieces were joined to make a complete mold.

The absence of molds for such objects as tankards or teapots suggests that they were never plentiful and that few, if any, were made in America. However, one advertisement of the nineteenth century has been

Hedderly & Riland's advertisement of "Pewterers' moulds made at the shortest notice." From Paxton's *Philadelphia Directory* for 1819. *Courtesy Historical Society of Pennsylvania*

HEDDERLY & RILAND,

Bell and Brass Founders, Smiths, &c.

NO. 134, S. FIFTH STREET, PHILADELPHIA,

Cast and hang Church, Ship, and House Bells, of any weight. Stair Rods, Andirons, and all kinds of brass work in general, made and repaired. Fan Sashes and Brackets made.

☞ *Pewterers' moulds made at the shortest notice.*

found which indicates the possibility of such molds having been made here, since the advertised production is not confined to spoon molds as in Thomas Gregory's advertisement. This notice appeared in Paxton's *Philadelphia Directory* for 1819, though the commodities included were probably of an eighteenth-century character:

> Hedderly and Riland, Bell and Brass Founders, Smiths, &c. Cast and hang Church, Ship, and House Bells, of any weight. Stair Rods, Andirons, and all kinds of brass work in general, made and repaired. Fan Sashes and Brackets made.
> *Pewterers' moulds made at the shortest notice.*

Doubtless other brass founders made molds; however, because of their exacting nature, their production must have been confined to highly skilled craftsmen familiar with the casting of pewter objects. Who polished, fitted, and hinged them is not known today.

The elusive metal molds of the eighteenth century were so costly that several pewterers often shared the use of one mold, and when new ones did come upon the market, there was no paucity of buyers for them. Because their high cost prohibited rapid changes in style, fashions in pewter objects changed slowly. Small spoon molds were more responsive to stylistic progression, but costly basin and tankard molds changed little throughout the time pewter objects were cast. As a matter of fact, there is not much evidence that styles in basins ever changed.

The use of the molds, the joining of parts, and the finishing of the objects will be described as these processes apply to the various products of the pewterer.

BUTTONS AND SPOONS

Casting Buttons

In casting pewter objects, there were technological problems to be solved in the use of each mold. Of them all, the use of the button mold required the least skill and knowledge. Still, there were certain precautions to be observed that were common to the use of all molds.

First, every mold had to be checked for tightness of fit and corrected, if need be. The high cost of molds made their long use a necessity, and inevitable wear often resulted in openings through which molten metal could leak. An accidental dropping of the mold in a bench or the floor could cause burrs which prevented parts from fitting neatly together.

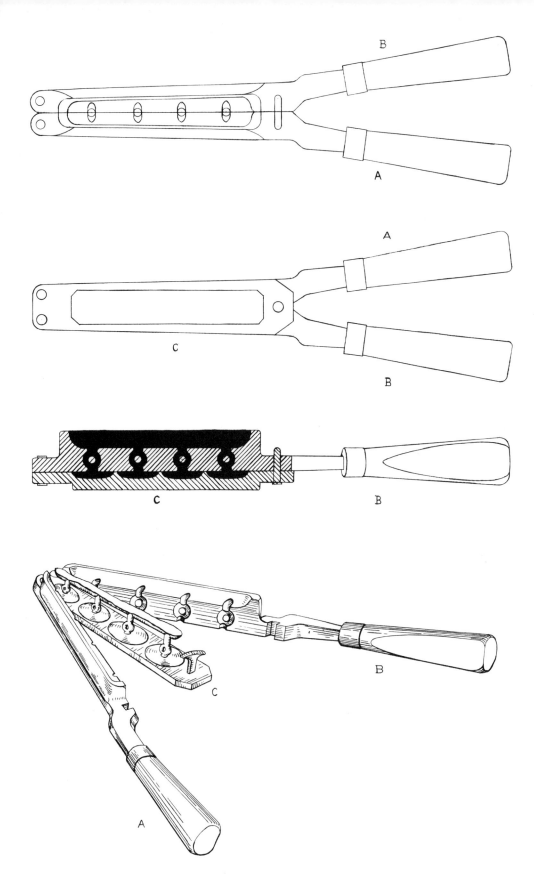

Mold for casting buttons. *Top to bottom*: Top view of closed mold. Bottom view of closed mold. Side view of mold showing cast buttons and trough filled with pewter. Mold opened, showing the casting of four buttons before removing them from the mold.

Second, the inner surfaces of the molds had to be protected from direct contact with the molten pewter. Bronze and brass have an affinity for tin-based metals and, unless a coating of some type was applied to keep the casting separate from the mold, the molten metal would turn casting and mold into one solid mass. An old recipe for a coating was egg white and red ochre. Often a coating of smoke (carbon) was completely adequate for the purpose, and molds have been found with remnants of smoke coating. A deposit of carbon could easily be applied by holding the mold over the flame of a candle or pine taper. Several castings could be made before a new application was necessary.

For the casting procedure, a reservoir of pewter was melted in an iron pot over a forge fire. The temperature of the molten metal was judged by placing the end of a pine taper in it and observing the charred surface which the molten metal produced. After the proper temperature was reached, the molten metal was poured into the mold through a trough-like opening at the top. The metal was then allowed to cool; small castings, such as buttons, required only a few minutes. Then the mold was opened and the casting carefully turned out onto a bench. When completely cooled, the excess metal, called a "sprue" or "tedge," was removed and the rough edges filed. Buttons were made smooth by rubbing them with cloth or leather to which oil and pumice powder had been applied. Sometimes buttons were covered with cloth like that of the garment on which it was sewed. Buttons ornamented with letters, such as U S A, were not covered; these are usually thought of as military buttons.

Casting Spoons

For the making of spoons, another fairly simple process, the first casting, as with buttons, were made in a cold mold. Only a few trial castings were required before the mold reached the optimum temperature for perfect castings. The thin cross-section of the bowl posed a problem not found in casting buttons; a more sensitive control of temperature was required or air pockets or "chills" would create an imperfect casting. Air pockets were eliminated by tapping the mold while the metal was still fluid. This tapping tended to eliminate chilled openings, too, but considerable experience was required to regularly produce perfect spoons.

How a two-piece mold was held in casting pewter spoons has always

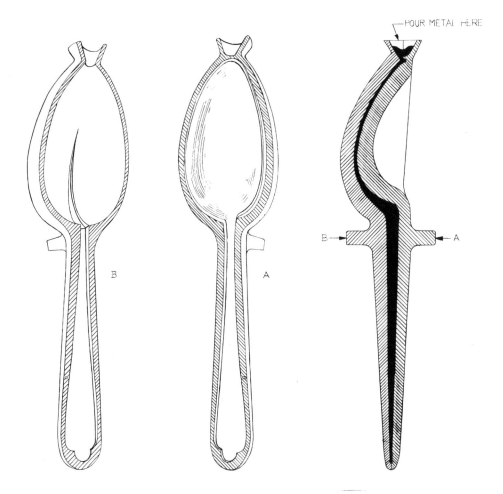

Mold used for casting spoons of pewter. *Top, left to right:* Inside view of a two-part mold; mold in position, showing casting in place. *Bottom:* Rack showing how molds were supported for the casting procedure. From *Cabinet Cyclopedia* by Rev. Dionysius Lardner

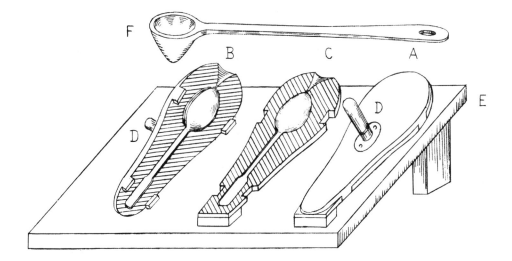

been somewhat of a mystery. A two-handled button mold could be conveniently held with one hand while the molten metal was poured with the other. With a two-piece spoon mold, where the parts were not attached to each other, some other plan had to be devised. Many spoon molds have a wooden handle on each half; one suspects they were held by the operator in both hands while another person poured the molten metal. Holding the halves of the mold together till they cooled might have been regarded as "busy work" for the apprentice.

A clever resolve of the problem is shown in a rare drawing in *The Cabinet Encyclopedia*, Volume III, by Rev. Dionysius Lardner (London, 1834), which illustrates how one man could perform this tedious operation. The directions ran:

> The annexed sketch represents two pairs of spoon moulds, which is generally the number managed by a single caster, the metal being left to cool a little in the one last filled while the spoon is removed, by means of a pair of pliers, from the other: *A* shows the mold closed up and ready for the reception of the metal by way of an orifice at the upper end; *B* and *C* are the two parts of another mould separated; *D D* are handles, by which the upper part of the mould is removed; *E E* is an inclined board fixed upon the workbench, near to where the caster sits, and within reach of the metal pot; *F* is the ladle, partly covered with a lid of sheet iron, which prevents the scum and dross from passing into the mould.
>
> After they [the spoons] come from the mould, they are scraped a little, stamped with the maker's name, and then polished, as we see them in the shops for sale.

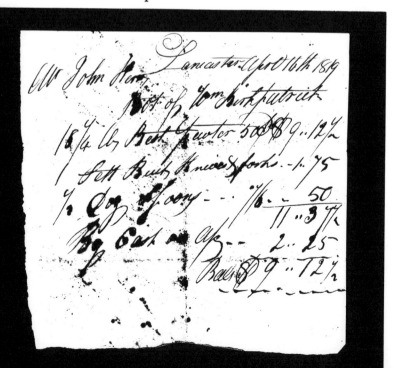

Invoice to Mr. John Herr of Lancaster, Pennsylvania, for pewter and utensils, from William Kirkpatrick. The balance indicates that credit-buying was practiced as early as 1819. *Kauffman collection*

A spoon mold was found in an attic in Pennsylvania with the halves attached to the jaws of a blacksmith's tongs, such as were used for holding hot metal while the blacksmith shaped it on his anvil. This discovery suggests that while molds with handles may have been used on a bench rack, as explained in the above quotation, those having short studs on each half were held by a pair of tongs.

The large number of spoon molds in collections today indicates a once brisk business in the making of pewter spoons. The fragility of the metal, the small size of the castings, and the considerable use to which such utensils were subjected would account for quick breakage or normal "wearing out" in a year or two, with a subsequent need for replacement. Probably a great many spoons were made by itinerants as they traveled through the countryside—a service they provided in addition to soldering leaking tin or copper utensils, oiling clocks, mending china, and other tinkering jobs. Very few spoons bear a maker's mark, though a few molds were engraved to enhance the esthetic appeal of the spoon beyond its functional contour.

BASINS AND PLATES

Next to spoon and button molds, plate molds have survived in greatest number in America, although, as has been pointed out, they are by no means plentiful. Perhaps a baker's half-dozen plate and a few basin molds can be found in the museums of the country; at least three are in private collections. The plates these molds produced range from eight to thirteen inches in diameter; some are shallow, others are deep.

It is noteworthy that most of the plate molds have been found in the South, particularly those at Old Salem, North Carolina. Their prevalence in the South is to some extent explained by the supposition that pewterware was used at a later date in the South than in the North, and molds, therefore, had a greater chance for survival there. It was also suggested that Northern economy moved discarded metal objects more vigorously to scrap yards from which they were fed into factories producing armaments and similar products.

All of the plate molds consist of two circular brass or bronze castings, mounted on iron strips which are hinged at one end and fitted with handles on the other. This arrangement permitted the two halves

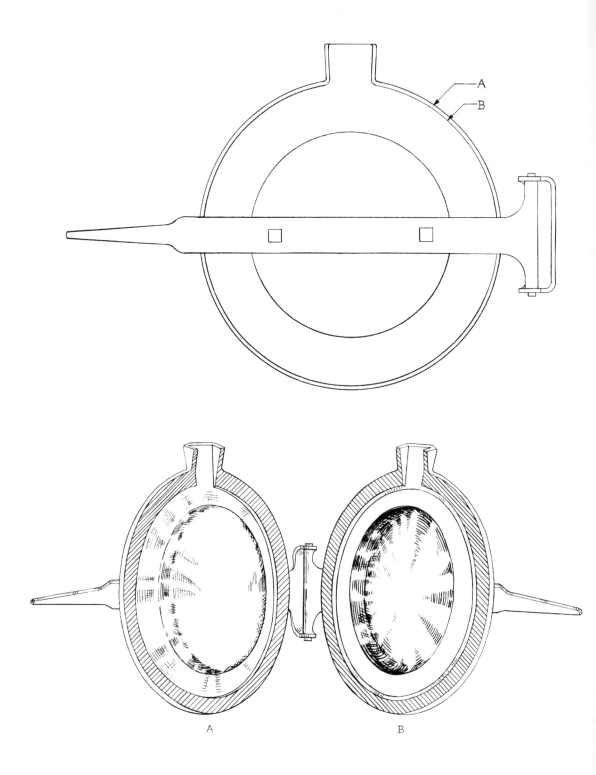

A   B

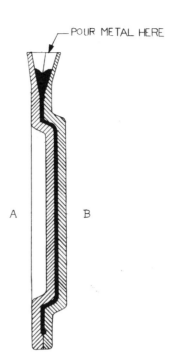

POUR METAL HERE

A   B

Plate molds. These varied in size, but the procedure
was essentially the same in all cases. *Top, opposite:*
Closed mold showing hinge and handle tangs; the
wooden handles are missing. *Bottom, opposite:* Mold
open showing the function of the protrusions at the
top of the mold where molten metal was poured in.
Right: Mold closed, showing the cast plate in position.

to be squeezed tightly together, so that the molten metal could not run
out between the castings while it was being poured. The precision in
fitting the two halves together is remarkable, particularly in the case
of large molds for plates and basins. Their outer diameter is about two
inches greater than that of the plate cast in them, and both sides have
half an ingate to form a gate or "tedge" on casting. This appendage is of
particular importance in the making of large castings, for as the molten
metal cools, it shrinks within the mold, and the reservoir of molten metal
provided in the tedge slowly drops into the cavity of the mold, keeping
it full as the metal shrinks.

Unlike the button and spoon molds, the plate mold was preheated
before casting the first plate. With the small molds only a few trial
castings were required to bring them up to proper working tempera-
tures, but to bring the large plate mold to its prime working temperature, many trial castings would have to be made. This preheating was
not only a matter of convenience, but a time-saver as well.

Possibly two plate molds were used simultaneously, as in the case of
spoon molds. The worker could be removing one plate as the metal in

Flat-rimmed pewter plate by William Will. The break in the plate between the rim and the booge is found more frequently on plates of American manufacture than on English plates. *Courtesy Philadelphia Museum of Art*

the other mold cooled. If the two parts of the mold fitted together properly, there was little excess metal around the edge to be removed. The tedge was removed by melting the metal with a soldering iron, or if small and thin, it was cut off with a pair of snips. Small holes were filled by melting scraps of pewter into them, and then scraping them smooth. Solder would have been easier to use, but the difference in color between solder and pewter would have spotted the surface of the plate.

Then came the impressing of the maker's mark on the top or bottom of the plate. Rarely was an American mark put on the rim as was often done in England, particularly in the seventeenth century. A steel die was used, engraved with the maker's name, or initials, and often with such symbols as eagles (in the nineteenth century) and geometric devices.

Before the plate was taken to the lathe for skimming and burnishing, the better craftsmen placed the plate upside down on a narrow round stake and hammered the booge (the round portion between the rim and the bottom) to make it more rigid. This procedure not only compacted the molecular structure of the metal, but also increased the esthetic appearance of the object.

The plate was ready then to be placed on a lathe for skimming the top surface with a scraping tool. The first step in this operation was to place a chuck of wood on a lathe to which a metal band was fastened, which extended forward far enough over the edge for one pewter plate to be attached to it. When the first plate was in place, the top surface was skimmed to eradicate any evidence of the casting process which might have been present. This metal tool had a long handle which the operator held under his arm; it was supported by a long tool-rest reaching from the headstock to the tailstock, parallel to the lathe bed and even in height with the center on the lathe. Power was provided either by the operator pressing a treadle with his foot or by an apprentice turning a large wheel. This was just one of the apprentice's tasks in acquiring the

Plate with the famous "Love" touchmark which is now universally regarded as the mark of an American craftsman living in the Philadelphia area in the late eighteenth century, despite the fact that virtually all such pieces have a London imprint. The mark consists of two doves with "LO" at one side and "VE" on the other. Many forms of vessels bear the mark of this man. *Kauffman collection*

experience and knowledge which would eventually lead to his journeyman-pewterer status.

After the top surface of the plate was skimmed, and it was reasonably smooth and the hammer marks on the inner side were removed, it was rubbed with a steel tool called a burnisher and finally, as the lathe rotated it, with a cloth or piece of leather charged with oil and rottenstone. When the inner surface of the first plate was finished, another plate was set atop it and skimmed and finished, so the plates piled up until the height of the pile complicated the procedure.

When the inner surfaces were finished, the plates were removed and placed bottoms up on the lathe and the bottom surfaces finished in the same fashion. The operator had to be careful not to remove the hammer marks on the outside of the booge, for these were evidence of careful craftsmanship and improved the value of the plate. He also took care not to remove the maker's mark, although it was often partially obliterated in the finishing process, or was probably not imprinted properly when the die was struck.

Occasionally the marks of the cutting tool or burnisher can be seen on plates which have not been used a great deal; these are not marks from spinning procedures as most people suspect.

Though casting and smoothing round plates was a tedious procedure, one of the pewterer's most complex problems arose when elliptical plat-

Basins vary in size and shape of rim. This one has a diameter of 5 ½ inches and bears the imprinted initials "T. D. & S. B." *Kauffman collection*

ters were made. There are no current hypotheses as to how the elliptical molds were made nor the castings finished. The work was done, though, and with considerable success, for few, if any, examples are found showing workmanship inferior to that on round objects.

Some pewter flatware with irregular shapes is believed to have been made from a thin cast sheet of pewter, which was hammered into shape. Extremely few examples of such work exist, and it has never been the writer's privilege to see one.

The procedures in casting a basin were essentially the same as those for casting a plate. The mold was hinged in a similar manner, the cooling probably required about the same time, but they were probably skimmed and burnished individually instead of stacking them on the lathe as was done with the plates.

INKSTANDS

To this point in the survey the directions for casting objects of pewter in bronze or brass molds have been concerned with a category of articles known as flatware, i.e., objects made of one piece of metal, such as plates, basins, or spoons. It has been pointed out that considerable skill and ingenuity were required to make the molds, but casting the objects of pewter required only a minimum of experience. In addition, because the objects consisted of only one piece, skills needed in assembling objects of more than one piece could be by-passed.

More skill, however, was required to cast and fabricate objects called hollow ware, i.e., objects made of more than one piece. Generally speaking, such objects were tall and cylindrical, with a bottom attached to make them watertight and usable, and usually with a handle and a lid. In the case of the tankard, all the above-named parts were required to make the object complete. Thus, in addition to using molds made up of many pieces, the various castings had to be fitted together so that joints were inconspicuous and the whole object was a harmonious assemblage from an esthetic point of view.

Possibly the simplest piece of hollow ware to make was an inkstand. The mold consisted of four parts, a top piece or cap, an inner core to make it hollow, and two sides called "cottles." The black portions in the cross-section represent the sections of the inkstand to be cast.

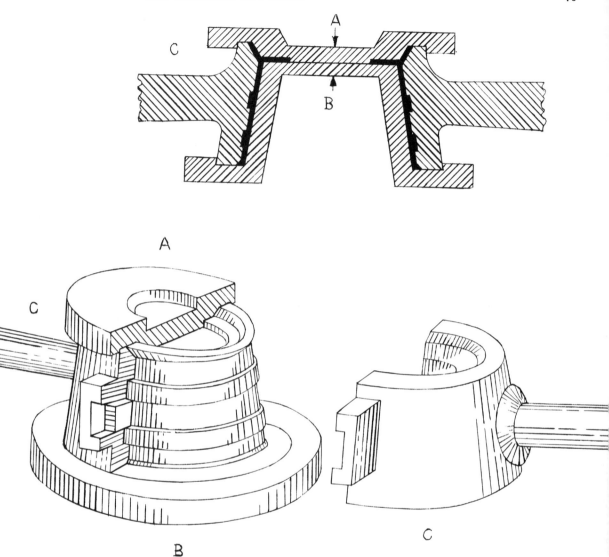

Molds for inkstands were cleverly fitted together so the proper places were allowed for the molten metal to flow, and so they could be disassembled easily to remove the casting. They were held together by a clamp or in a vise. *Top:* Mold for inkstand assembled, with the casting in place. *Bottom:* Mold partially disassembled, showing the protrusion where the metal was poured in to fill the cavity.

When the mold was put together and inward pressure applied with a clamp to the top and bottom portions, the assembled parts fitted tightly and rigidly. It was then laid on its side, filled through the tedge and allowed to cool until the metal became solid. The top part of the mold was knocked off with a mallet and, while the mold was held in the hand, the bottom was struck to remove the inner part, or core. The two cottles were then pulled apart by their handles, and the casting removed from the one half to which it happened to stick fast. Great care was required to prevent breaking this thin hollow casting.

It is evident that the casting of the inkstand was complete except for a thin sheet of metal needed to enclose the bottom opening. This thin sheet could be easily cast between two flat pieces of metal and cut slightly larger (by about one-eighth inch in diameter) than the diameter of the bottom of the inkstand. Soldering such joints was frowned upon by professionals for, after oxidation, the solder produced a narrow gray line which distinguished it from the color of the pewter. A discriminating buyer of the eighteenth century would not have bought an inkstand having a bottom attached with solder.

A blown-glass ink container was fitted into the opening left at the top of the inkstand, and holes were made around the container for holding quill pens. Large inkstands had covers hinged to the top to protect the ink from evaporation and from debris falling into it. After filing and polishing, the inkstand was ready for sale and use.

Inkstand fabricated of flat sheets with a vertical plate through the middle to which the lid hinges are attached. This one bears the imprint of Henry Will, who is thought to have worked in New York City from 1736 to 1802. *Courtesy The Brooklyn Museum*

The description and directions for making a round inkstand should not lead the reader to believe that none but round ones were made. A number of small, shallow, rectangular boxes, about 4½ by 7½ inches, longitudinally divided into two equal parts with a hinged lid on each part, served also as inkstands. One half of the box was undivided, presumably for quills when not in use, while the other half was divided into three parts, one for an inkwell, another for sand used in blotting the ink, and the center portion presumably reserved for a seal and sealing wax. Twenty years ago unmarked objects of this type were easily obtained, and because only one example bore the mark of an American craftsman (Henry Will), it was generally assumed that most of them were of English origin. In retrospect, this deduction does not seem very valid now, but such was the case when they were available. Today, extremely few of this type can be found in the antique shops of America.

A close examination of one of these boxes suggests that the flat sheets of which it was made were cast, and the form assembled by fusing or soldering the various parts together. The containers for ink and sand were easily removed for use or filling.

It is very interesting to note that one oval standish (inkstand) was listed in the Byles inventory. Such an item would be regarded as a great rarity by collectors today.

BEAKERS AND MUGS

Although the form of the beaker appears to have some historical precedent, i.e., it is essentially the shape of a tapering cup made from a section of an animal's horn, it must be noted that the etymology of the word is very brief. As a matter of fact, it does not seem to have evolved from earlier words in English or other languages describing a similar object. Most references, such as dictionaries and encyclopedias, describe a beaker as a wide-mouthed vessel used for drinking or laboratory purposes. The latter concept must obviously be of recent origin, and as drinking vessels they are not among the oldest vessels used for this pur-

---

Although no molds for beakers survive, it is likely that the shape of the mold and the casting techniques resembled those used in making inkstands, the handle excepted. *Top:* Assembled mold showing the casting in place. *Bottom:* Partially disassembled mold showing the separation of the two outer halves.

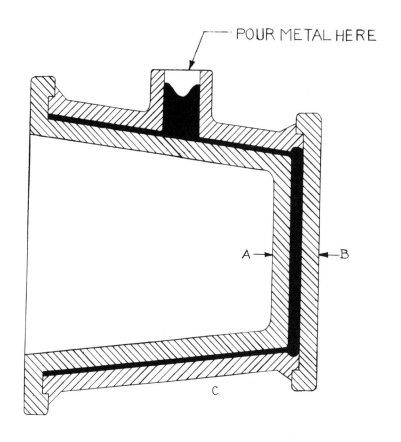

POUR METAL HERE

A   B

C

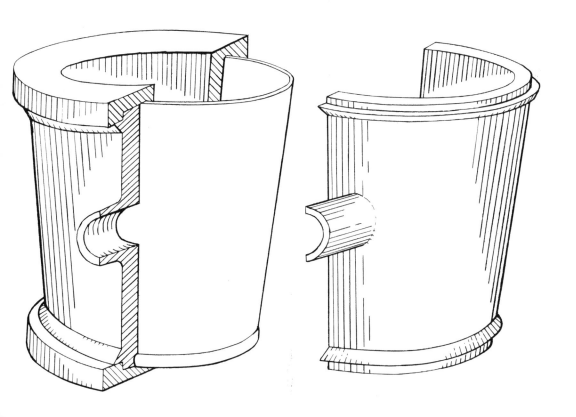

SEPARATE HERE

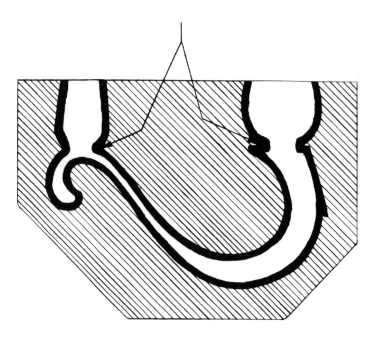

Section of a beaker mold used to "slush" cast the hollow handle (the same procedure with a larger mold was used to form the handles for mugs). Beaker is about 3 inches high.

pose in America; however, some were made here of pewter in the eighteenth century. Those of earliest type are usually tall and were made by such outstanding craftsmen as John Bassett and Samuel Danforth. A shorter type, possibly four inches tall, was made by a number of craftsmen in the nineteenth century. Ashbil Griswold marked a number of his short beakers with an intaglio stamp creating his initials, "A. G.," in a small rectangle on the bottom.

Regardless of the history, the size, the utility, or the marking of these objects, a consideration of beakers at this point is indicated by the fact that many of them were made in the tradition of the eighteenth century; that is, they were formed by the casting process. An examination of many made in the nineteenth century confirms the fact that some of them were also cast in the later era.

It may seem illogical to deal with the making of a beaker after the discussion of the inkstand, for the latter was obviously more difficult to make, being composed of more than one piece, while many beakers

were not; however, the making of the handle on the beaker illustrated
introduced a new and reasonably complicated procedure, which really
demanded more skill than was required for the making of an inkstand.

The mold for the common beaker closely resembles the one for the
casting of an inkstand. It consisted of an inner core which created the
hollow interior of the beaker, two outer cottles which confined the
molten metal to the desired exterior shape and size, and a cap, or top
disc, which completely confined the molten metal to the desired cavity
and held the two cottles together at the one end. The inner core held
the cottles together at the other end. By applying pressure against the
two ends by clamps in a vise the entity was held together and ready for
the pouring of the metal into the ingate.

Only a few minutes were needed for the metal to solidify, after which
the mold could be disassembled. The casting, although different in pro-
portion from the inkstand, was a thin shell with a bottom, while the
round inkstand had a top and an opening to receive the glass container
for ink. They were also inverted when in use, the large diameter of the
beaker being the top, while the large diameter of the inkstand was the
bottom.

The tedge was subsequently removed and the beaker fitted to a form
on the lathe for skimming and burnishing. Various arrangements of lines
were often cut into the beaker as it revolved on the lathe, none of which
obviously were cut through the shell, or the beaker would leak. The
molded edge on the bottom was shaped to create an appropriate base,
and undercut on the very bottom to provide an even footing on which
the beaker stood. The final polishing and burnishing concluded the work
on most beakers; however, the one described here has a handle, which
created a number of problems not met in the making of a beaker without this useful appendage.

Although it is quite evident that most beakers do not have handles,
the fact that some do cannot be ignored, and, therefore, the mode of
making the handles must be explained. Not only did the making of these
handles involve one of the "trickiest" operations in the making of
pewter vessels, but the same operations was also used to produce the
handles on most mugs and the spouts on all teapots.

The problem that confronted the pewterer was to create a hollow
part. In the case of the handle, the intent was to reduce the weight of

Two very rare beakers by Johann Christopher Heyne of Lancaster, Pennsylvania. These were doubtless used for serving wine in a communion service for a small congregation. *Bottom:* "ICH" imprint *Courtesy The Historical Society of York County, Pa.*

the part; and it is very obvious that the spout had to be hollow to perform its function. One would logically conclude that these parts could have easily been made of sheet pewter, as they were in silver; however, the low malleability of pewter did not permit such a procedure to be followed. Thus, some alternative method had to be devised.

The method used required that two pieces of metal, probably brass or bronze, be fitted together broadside, and that within the joined parts a cavity be created the exact shape and size of the desired part. In order to avoid a binding action on either of the parts, the separation had to occur exactly in the middle of the casting. The creation of these parts was a common foundry procedure; the only precautions necessary were that the parts fit tightly together and that pins or notches be provided in each part so they could be reassembled perfectly each time after they had been parted to remove the casting. The cavity within had to be covered with smoke (carbon) to prevent the casting from sticking to the mold.

To cast the desired part, the two pieces of metal were held tightly together by a clamp and molten pewter was poured into the cavity until it was filled. Close observation discloses that the hot metal quickly solidified around the edges when poured into the cold mold, and while

Beaker, probably the product of an American craftsman, with a handle similar to those used on pint and quart mugs and tankards. *Kauffman collection*

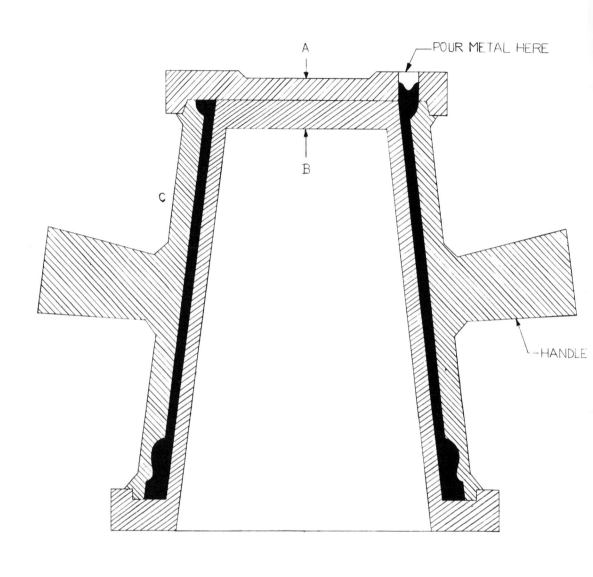

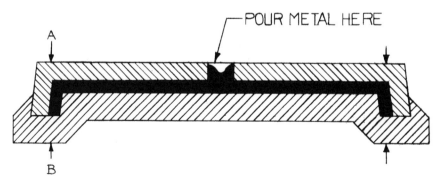

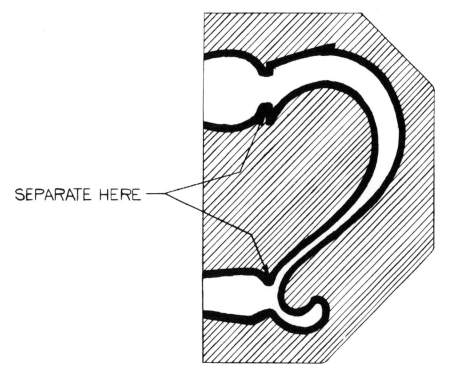

SEPARATE HERE

It is obvious that a straight-sided mug resembled the shape of an inverted beaker. The fact that the bottom was in the large end required that the bottom be cast separately and inserted later. *Top, opposite:* Section of a four-piece mold for a mug with the casting in place. *Bottom, opposite:* Two-piece mold for casting bottoms for mugs. *Above:* Section of mold for "slush" casting the handle.

the inner portion of the pewter was still fluid, the mold was quickly turned upside down so that the inner section, or core, could flow out, thus creating a hollow casting. This method was called "slush" casting. Imperfections were apt to occur at the mouth of the openings; for this reason, extra portions were created there which were later removed. Thus, a casting unimpaired as to size and shape could be fitted to the side of the beaker.

In addition to the fitting to the beaker, the surface of the handle had to be made smooth and finished, for this procedure was easier to accomplish before the handle was attached than afterward. When the beaker and the handle were ready for assembly, they were "fitted and fluxed," and solder was applied and heated until it flowed into its proper locations. It was very essential that all parts contacted each other at all points, for solder flows by capillary action, and would not flow if all parts did not fit perfectly together.

A survey of sentiment among collectors of pewter indicates that the pewter tankard, like its silver counterpart, was the aristocrat among household and tavern vessels. Obviously, since not everyone could afford the flourish of a fine lid and ornamented thumbpiece, the less fortunate had to be satisfied with a lidless vessel, variously described as a mug or pot. The name "mug" is commonly used today, but it is reported that in colonial inventories they were also listed as "pots."

The term "pot" is rarely used today for such a vessel and a survey of references indicates that it was never solely applied to articles made of pewter or silver. *An American Dictionary of the English Language,* Springfield, Massachusetts, 1848, provides a definition of a pot as contemporary society views the object:

> 1. A vessel more deep than broad, made of earth, or iron, or other metal, used for several domestic purposes as, an iron *pot* for boiling meat or vegetables; a *pot* for holding liquors; a cup as, a *pot* of ale, i.e., a quart.

One might question the fact that all mugs or pots held a quart of liquid since many with a pint capacity were also made.

The point should be made that, in addition to their function as vessels for drinking, they were used as measures; in fact, the capacity of many English examples is stamped on them near the top edge. On later examples the capacity is indicated on the side near the middle, often in a "block" type of lettering which is not very attractive. Some of those used in taverns are stamped with a date, indicating that a sealer of weights and measures had made periodic visits to check the capacity to make sure that the public was not being cheated. Few American examples are stamped with the capacity of the vessel, and the writer has never seen one bearing the date stamp of the sealer of weights and measures.

Most American examples have straight sides. Of the twenty-three illustrated by Ledlie Laughlin in *Pewter in America,* all but four are of this shape. One vessel has a bulbous-shaped body and a "double-C" handle, ornamented on top with an acanthus-leaf decoration. This piece is probably unique, although the writer owns a sugar bowl, made by a Philadelphia craftsman, with a similar leaf ornamentation on the handles. To further complicate the terminology applied to these vessels, it must be noted that silver vessels of this bulbous shape were called "canns." Some people apply the same name to a similar vessel made of pewter.

Quart-sized pewter mug by Thomas Danforth. The "off-pewter" color of this vessel is due to the fact that it was silver-plated many years ago. *Kauffman collection*

Parks Boyd, also of Philadelphia, made at least one mug in the shape of a barrel and Robert Palethorp, of the same city, fashioned one with a modified barrel shape.

The procedures in making a straight-sided mug varied from those followed in producing a beaker because the location of the bottom of the beaker permitted the entire body to be cast in a single mold. The fact that the mug flared in the opposite direction did not permit a similar technique in its making. The position of the bottom in the wide end of the mug required that the body and the bottom be cast separately, after which the two parts were cleverly fitted together so that they appeared to have been made of one piece. A narrow ledge was cast around the edge of the bottom, so that when it was inserted into the body, the edge (and not the bottom) of the vessel touched the top of the table. This procedure was probably followed so that, if the bottom became uneven, the mug continued to sit flat on the table. In more modern times such a facility would also be very convenient as a secret place for leaving a tip for the "barmaid." Mugs with bottoms of glass are strictly a modern invention.

The procedures used in making mugs with bulbous-shaped bodies will be found in the directions for making similarly shaped tankards. The same molds were probably used to make the bodies of both vessels; in the case of the tankard, however, a lid and thumbpiece were added.

Some mugs made by Nathaniel Austin of Charlestown, Massachusetts, and Gershom Jones of Providence, Rhode Island, have handles made of strips of pewter with a minimum of ornamentation. These handles were formed of a solid piece of metal and soldered to the body of the mugs. Most mugs have hollow handles, cast in one solid piece by the "slush" method used to cast the handle for the beaker. All handles were fitted and polished before they were attached with solder in the traditional way.

Little ornamentation is found on pewter mugs. It was noted that an acanthus leaf was applied to one handle, but the traditional decoration consisted of a wide band at the bottom edge and a narrow one at the top. These additions made the terminal points more rigid and attractive. Many have medial bands, usually located a bit above or below the center, and a few were ornamented with engraved designs. An interesting example is one, by an unknown American craftsman, that features a horse and rider, combined with lettering.

TANKARDS, FLAGONS, AND MEASURES

It has been pointed out that the bodies of mugs and tankards were similar in shape throughout the eighteenth century. The straight-sided, flat-lidded tankard held sway among producers in the early part of the century, later joined by the tulip-shape, the latter with a "double-C" scroll handle and a concave molded base, but the simple straight-sided style seems to have never been completely discarded as long as tankards were made. The lid of the straight-sided tankard did change, usually to a double-domed shape, and there were variations in thumbpieces. Although the illustrations appearing in *Pewter in America* may not present a true relationship of the ratio in numbers, it should be noted that twenty-two tankards with straight sides are illustrated, while only two of the type with bulbous bodies (tulip-shape) are shown. The large number of tankards illustrated also attests to the importance of these objects, for only mugs are also illustrated in so great a number.

Straight-sided tankard by William Will of Philadelphia, Pennsylvania. With the exception of the thumbpiece and the lid, this vessel was obviously similar to a mug. Directions for casting the lid are included in the data about the tankard with a bulbous-shaped body. 7 inches high. *Courtesy Philadelphia Museum of Art*

Because the making of the body of a straight-sided tankard is similar to that type of mug, the reader is referred to the discussion of mugs for this information. It is the author's belief that in many cases the high cost of the molds necessitated that the same one be used for both objects. The fact that William Will is one of the few craftsmen to produce mugs ("canns"), and tankards with bulbous bodies suggests that he used the same mold for both objects.

Directions for the making of a lid, handle, and thumbpiece can be found in the description, which follows, of the forming of a tulip-shaped tankard; so the shape of the lid on the early straight-sided type is the major design facet to be considered here.

The evolution of the design seems to have followed logical steps. One would naturally suppose the first lid on such an object to be composed

Two views of a straight-sided tankard made by Henry Will of New York City. This one is distinguished because of the serrated border on the front side of the lid. 7 inches high. *Kauffman collection*

of a flat piece of metal with a simple facility, such as a thumbpiece and hinge, to raise it. A flat piece being not very ornamental nor very rigid, the craftsman gave the part a contour which was a step away from its original simplicity and which, at the same time, increased its rigidity. The main surfaces remained flat, but the center portion was raised with a curved booge between the inner and outer flat surfaces. A similar procedure probably occurred in making objects of both silver and pewter, but the change was more significant in objects of pewter, for this metal could be more easily distorted than could silver. Tankards with so-called flat tops (the center portion being raised but flat) represent the oldest style executed in America and are generally regarded as the most desirable to own. The bodies of the early straight-sided vessels were rather low and broad, a ratio found in very few mugs. Since the capacity of most tankards was either a pint or a quart, a three and one-half pint tankard by Francis Bassett stands among the rarities in this field.

Another logical step in the evolution of styles of lids was to make a dome form (the first such style is described as a single dome) which was succeeded by a double-domed pattern with intersecting flat bands, which added to the attractive appearance of the part. The transition was slow; an example of this single-domed style by Henry Will displays a lid which is really neither flat nor domed. Finally, the attractive double-domed style evolved, reaching the zenith in lid designs for tankards; a few have turned finials similar to those found on fine silver tankards, but not as highly ornamented as were the silver.

Most of the early thumbpieces were compatible as a whole with the simplicity of the vessel. A corkscrew pattern was used, which was easy to cast and finish with hand methods. Among tankards with flat tops a few pierced examples are also found, although this feature was more frequently used on examples made after the middle of the century.

Flat-top tankard. Will's touch appears on inside bottom; same touch is used in his teapot. *Courtesy John J. Evans, Jr.*

It has been pointed out by earlier writers that the division between domestic and ecclesiastical vessels is strictly an arbitrary one. It is evident in some cases, however, that certain objects were made for specific use in the home. In the case of the flagon it is highly improbable, from the writer's point of view, that this vessel was intended for domestic use. Many congregations could not have afforded a flagon, for they must have been costly; often, then, for Holy Communion services tankards were substituted. Sometimes they were bought for this purpose, while at other times they were gifts from members of the congregation, as were frequently all of the vessels used for communion. It is a curious paradox that in some cases the same form served for dispensing liquids in taverns and in churches.

Flagons are considered in the same category with tankards because in reality they were only enlarged (principally taller) tankards. A few, however, have spouts, which virtually no American tankard had when it was made. It is not uncommon to find tankards with spouts, but usually the spouts are later additions. The similarity between flagons and tankards is so real that some of the parts were used on both vessels. The most handsome flagon illustrated in *Pewter in America* is marred only by the fact that it has a normal tankard handle instead of the larger flagon handle, which was often made up of parts of two tankard handles. Most flagons have a decorative band, placed either above or below the center, to relieve the plainness which their height accentuates.

Although many flagons are straight-sided, the sides flare outward, creating a greater diameter at the bottom than at the top. This design was not only esthetically pleasing, it simplified the process of making the bodies because they could be made in a single mold. The famous flagons made by Johann Christopher Heyne of Lancaster, Pennsylvania, have a distinct curved flare at the bottom, but they could have been cast in a single mold. The bottom was usually made of a thin cast piece of pewter; however, the ingenious Heyne used a standard six-inch plate for

This communion flagon with a strap handle was made by a German craftsman and was used by the congregation of Trinity Lutheran Church in Lancaster, Pennsylvania, until additional ones were made by Heyne. *Courtesy Trinity Lutheran Church*

Communion flagon by Johann Christopher Heyne. *Left:* The bottom was made from Heyne's mold for six-inch plates. Such plates are extant and bear an imprint similar to the one found on the bottom of the flagon. *Right:* Heyne's use of an English handle created a problem in placing the thumbpiece, but he made a clever adaptation. The handle, however, is a tankard type and is too small for the vessel. The feet made in the form of cherubs' heads are a typical German procedure. 12 inches high. *Courtesy Trinity Lutheran Church, Lancaster, Pennsylvania*

the bottom of his flagons. His early thumbpiece was a ball in the true Germanic tradition, which was easy to make; later, he did adopt a typical English thumbpiece as well as other English patterns.

The production of flagons appears to have involved the same procedures used in making a tankard. The larger size of the vessel increased the chances for failure, for the mold was more difficult to heat uniformly than was the smaller one for a tankard, and the possibility of chills and other hazards was greater in casting the larger vessels. The handle was made by the "slush" casting method, polished and soldered in place along with the hinge and the thumbpiece.

The making of the tulip-shaped tankard might logically follow the data about the straight-sided tankard; but because of the similarity in

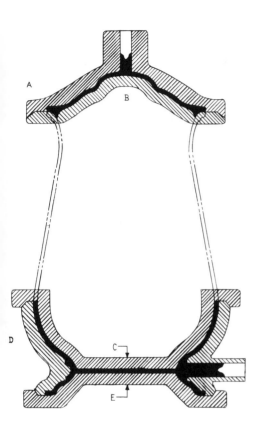

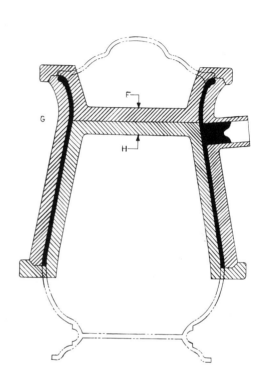

Bulbous-bodied tankards with "double-C" scroll handles and a thumbpiece required quite a number of molds. *Top, left:* Molds for lids and bottoms with the castings in place; they were held together in a vise or by clamps for the casting process. *Top, right:* Molds for casting the upper portion of the body; the procedure was very similar to the casting of the round inkstand. *Bottom:* The mold for the body partially disassembled.

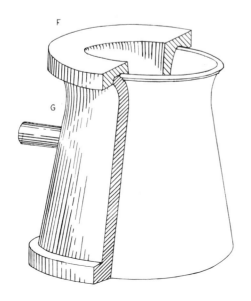

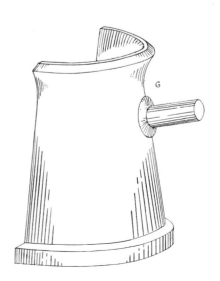

Mold for "slush" casting the
"double-C" handle. A separate
mold was needed to cast the
thumbpiece.

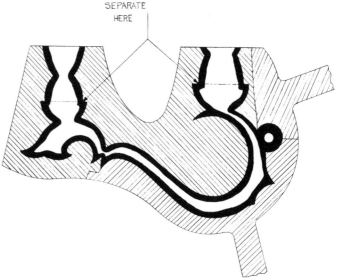

SEPARATE
HERE

molds and methods used in making a straight-sided tankard and a flagon,
the tulip-shaped tankard is in a category of its own because of the com-
plexity of the technological problems involved in its making. Five molds
were needed to make this uniquely shaped vessel, two of which each
had four parts.

The problem of production is complicated largely by the fact that
there are virtually no straight portions in the object, that there were no
simple flaring parts, and that, after the parts were cast, they had to be
assembled to appear to be an integral unit. The process is somewhat similar to the fabrication of a body for a modern automobile. Many parts
must be made separately but the final product must appear to have been
created by the swoop of one massive tool.

The multiplicity of the parts, and the problems created in fitting them
together, must have challenged the skill and ingenuity of the most clever
craftsman. It is obvious that casting the lid was a relatively simple procedure, similar to the casting of the bottom for the mug. It had to be
skimmed on the lathe and virtually finished before it was ready to become an integral part of the total assembly.

The handle of the tulip-shaped tankard was cast by the "slush"
method used to cast the handle for the beaker, mug, and flagon, but in

this case the problem was additionally complicated by the fact that knuckles for the hinge of the thumbpiece had also to be formed as part of the handle. A separate mold was used for casting the thumbpiece; then the lid, thumbpiece, and handle had to be meticulously fitted so they functioned properly and made an attractive appearance.

The work on these smaller parts was tedious and required patience and skill; however, the casting of the body was possibly the most critical procedure in making this tankard. The molds had not only to be made so the castings were the correct size and shape when they were produced, but also the two major parts of the body had to appear as a single unit after they were joined. Because the joint was located at the most conspicuous part of the vessel the fit had to be as perfect and as unnoticeable as possible.

After both parts of the body were skimmed on the lathe they were "butted" against each other and fused (welded) together with the very metal from which they were cast. It would have been much easier to join

Quart tankard with tulip-shaped body; made by William Will. This is an attractive example of this type of tankard, particularly with the piercing in the shape of a heart in the thumbpiece.
Courtesy The Brooklyn Museum

the two parts with solder; however, on oxidation, the solder would have created a thin gray line around the perimeter of the tankard, particularly if they were not polished regularly. The workmanship on this joint was usually executed with such skill that it cannot be detected on the outside, and often is difficult to find on the inside of the tankard.

After the two parts of the body were joined and the excess metal removed at the joint, the surface was polished, particularly the area under the handle where access became almost impossible after the handle was attached.

A close examination of a measure immediately reveals that the body was fabricated in a way very similar to that of the tulip-shaped tankard. The body was cast in two parts and joined about in the middle, or at least the greatest diameter. The parts of the body were skimmed and joined as described for the tulip-shaped tankard; however, the handle was solid and attached by an entirely different method.

A two-piece mold with a cavity the shape of the desired handle was formed and fitted to the surface of the measure as indicated in the accompanying illustration. Molten metal was poured into the mold, but instead of pouring the inside portion of the metal out before it solidified entirely, the whole unit was allowed to solidify, and only the ingate had

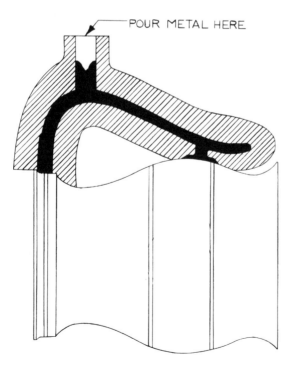

POUR METAL HERE

SECTION

Two-piece mold for casting the handle for a measure. This was a solid handle and was not cast by the "slush" method. After the handle solidified, the mold was removed.

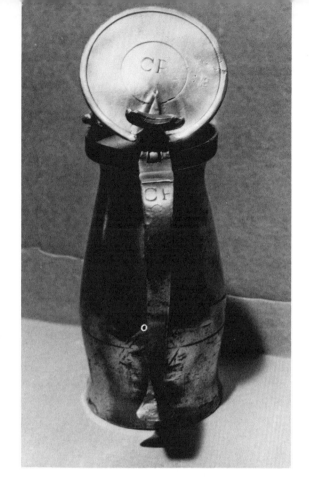

Unmarked quart measure, thought to be the product of an American craftsman. The "CP" was imprinted at a Philadelphia "proof house" and presumably stands for "City (of) Philadelphia." *Kauffman collection*

to be removed and the handle polished. Most measures have a "linen mark" on the inside where the handle is attached. It is usually easily seen at the top, but often very obscure at the point where the bottom end of the handle is attached.

It should be noted that marked American measures are among the rarest of American forms. A few are extant bearing Boardman touches, but none by other makers are known to exist.

COFFEEPOTS AND TEAPOTS

The perceptive observer of trends in collecting American pewter has doubtless noticed a turn of events which was predicted by John W. Poole in 1940. At that time most serious collectors wanted to fill their mantles and cupboards with tankards, often bypassing the exquisite teapots of the eighteenth century, which were rarer and equally attractive. At the present time it cannot be said that tankards have lost much of their glamor, but it can be claimed that the luster of teapots and coffeepots has certainly become brighter.

A number of craftsmen made teapots in the Queen Anne style. They had a charming shape; they were practical to use; and they were compatible with contemporary styles in other pieces. *Top:* This pot is unusual because it has "hoof-type" feet. *Kauffman collection. Bottom:* A similar style made by William Will, but without feet. *Courtesy The Brooklyn Museum*

Another example of a Queen Anne teapot by William Will, but an indiscreet owner removed half of the legs. *Courtesy Philadelphia Museum of Art*

An examination of the parts of a charming Queen Anne (pear-shaped) teapot reveals that they were made in a manner very similar to that of the tulip-shaped tankard, with a few exceptions. The lid was cast in a two-piece mold to which a finial was added. A ring of wood was usually inserted in the finial as a comfortable fingerhold due to its low conductivity of heat from the contents of the pot. This contingency was, of course, not important in the making and using of a tankard. The handle was also made of wood and attached to the body by the use of two round tennons pinned into flaring cylinders on the side of the body opposite the spout. The spout was made in the traditional manner for making "slush" castings.

The body of the pot was cast in two molds; however, it should be noted that a base was not included in the mold for the bottom part. The castings were skimmed on the lathe and then joined by fusing small chips of pewter where the two parts met. The technology of the construction required that the joint be placed at the greatest diameter of the pot.

Instead of a concave band of metal for the base as the tankard had, cabriole legs were often used, terminating in "ball and claw" or "hoof" feet; however, some teapots of this type did not have any legs or feet. A teapot made by Cornelius Bradford of Philadelphia and New York City has the more unusual "hoof" feet.

Such legs and feet were a very attractive feature of a teapot and were doubtless very functional in disseminating heat from the contents of the pot before it reached the top of the table. They were probably cast in plaster molds from models of wood or wax, and needed little finishing before they were attached to the body of the pots.

Teapot in the drum form used by a number of silversmiths in the late eighteenth century. This one bears the "Love" imprint; that and the beaded edges of the lid and the body of the pot suggest it was produced in the Philadelphia area. *Formerly in the Kauffman collection*

Although it was a very natural and attractive procedure to have the top half of the teapot different from the bottom, it was not until the nineteenth century that Thomas D. Boardman adapted the contour of the parts so that one shape could be used for both the top and the bottom. The shape he evolved could have been either cast or spun; however, it is likely that they were at first cast. A precedent for such a procedure is found in the making of a dram bottle by Heyne at the time of the American Revolution. Curiously, the balance of Boardman's form continues the Queen Anne tradition, except that the handle was made of metal ("slush" cast) instead of wood as in the earlier pots.

Doubtlessly influenced by teapots made by silversmiths in a drum form, it would be very logical for the pewterers to follow suit; however, this form is very rare in pewter. William Will and Love are known to have made this style with a straight tapering spout, a handle of wood, but without legs. The beaded edges betray their Philadelphia produc-

Tall coffeepot (15¾ inches high) by William Will. This is the only form of coffeepot known to have survived from the eighteenth century. Its form appears to be derived from the Queen Anne style, but greatly stretched in height from a teapot to a coffeepot. It has five rings of beads which add considerably to its appearance and value. *Courtesy Henry Francis du Pont Winterthur Museum*

tion, which was used on other objects made by a number of makers who worked there.

Coffeepots made in America in the eighteenth century are extremely scarce. In the first place, coffee was originally cultivated and used by the Turks in the seventeenth century where it was a very popular drink because their religion forbad the use of alcohol. It was made from a berry as black as soot and as bitter; but the Turks found that it helped digestion and promoted alacrity. A Greek servant of a Turkish merchant opened the first coffeehouse in London in 1652, the first in England being opened a year before at Oxford. Within twenty years, the first coffeehouse in America was founded in Boston.

The term "coffeepot" implies that the brew was boiled in the pot, but such a procedure was not possible in a vessel made of pewter. It was obviously prepared in another container and then placed in the pewter coffeepot for serving.

No urns were used in the eighteenth century for serving coffee and only a few pots were apparently made by William Will. Their height over-all is 15¾ inches, the bottom diameter 4½ inches, top diameter 3⅜ inches, and the greatest width of the bowl is 6 inches. The spout is long and small in diameter; the body slightly resembles the shape of a Queen Anne teapot which had been stretched vertically from its original height. The beaded edges are evidence of production in Philadelphia, and it must have been cast from molds designed for such an unusual piece. Extremely few of them have survived. The scarcity of coffeepots was of short duration in America for the first half of the nineteenth century was labeled the "Coffeepot Era" by J. B. Kerfoot who compiled a list of sixty-four makers who worked at that time (*American Pewter*). It is not presumed, however, that all of them made coffeepots.

PORRINGERS

Although there is some variation in the shape and style of silver porringers, it can be said that the greatest diversity is in the pattern of the handles. And, despite the dissimilarities, there is a consistency in the planned relationship of the pierced patterns and the outer contours of the handles, which range from a few large openings in some to a profusion of small openings in others.

The situation is different in the style of porringers made of pewter, for in these there are two distinct and separate styles. The differences in these two styles are pronounced, for one is very similar to those made of silver while the other can be described as unique to those made of pewter.

The most interesting aspect in the making of the pewter porringer resembling in style those of silver lies in the making of the bowl. It is quite obvious that the bowl is cast, and one can readily imagine the exterior shape being formed by an outer mold made of two pieces, which could be easily joined and separated, as in the making of other objects of pewter. The inner mold would doubtless have to be segmented in some way so that it could be disassembled for removal, since the top diameter of the porringer is smaller than that of the body at its greatest width.

Of course, the whole inner core could have been made in sand. This inner core of sand could have been baked hard and centered in an outer case of metal. Or the entire mold could have been made of sand, each

The function of porringers is rather uncertain; however, the name implies that they were used to serve porridge. This early English example may have been used for "bloodletting." The lines on the inside may have indicated the quantity of blood taken from the patient. *Courtesy Philadelphia Museum of Art*

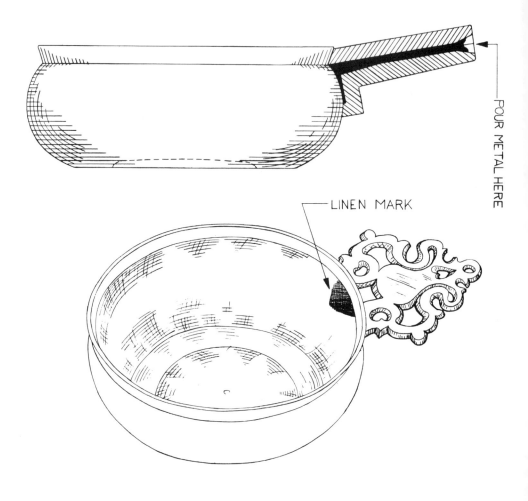

A two-piece mold was fitted to the exterior shape of the porringer and the molten metal poured in as indicated in the drawing. *Top:* The two-piece mold in place, showing the cast metal. *Bottom:* The "linen mark" on the inside of the bowl.

casting requiring the making of a separate mold; after the casting, the complete mold would have been destroyed. It is the belief of the writer, however, that the entire casting was made in metal molds, as were other objects of pewter in the eighteenth century. One such possibility could be that the body was cast in halves and the two joined to make a complete bowl. However, it has never been reported that evidence of such a joint has ever been detected in the bowl; thus this hypothesis is not

Top: An example showing that the pattern did not fit perfectly and excess metal "ran out" between the mold and the bowl of the porringer. *Bottom:* The top surface of the same porringer was never made smooth. The bowl is the only finished part of the porringer. About 4 inches in diameter. *Kauffman collection*

seriously considered as the solution of the problem. Other hypotheses might be advanced for this mysterious procedure, but at the moment, none seems to be logical.

The bodies of the porringers were skimmed and polished on a lathe before the handle was attached, and the mode of attaching the handle is perhaps one of the most bizarre and interesting techniques of the whole trade. A two-piece mold was fitted to the exterior contour of the bowl of the porringer, and a pad of linen was held against the inside of the bowl at the point where the handle was to be attached. After all fittings and precautions were carefully attended to, molten metal was poured into the top of the handle mold, which flowed down against the exterior surface of the porringer. The molten metal for the handle "slushed" the metal of the bowl in a small area, and the two parts were united without the use of solder. The "slushed" condition of the metal caused the linen pad, held inside the bowl, to make an imprint in the metal, which is found in virtually all "period" porringers. This imprint is commonly called a "linen mark."

The various openings in the handles were formed by the mold at the time of the casting, a different mold being needed for each style of

Two-piece mold for a porringer with the handle cast with the bowl, showing the casting in place. The number of porringer forms and decorative details seems endless, but next in importance to the type with a rounded bowl is the basin-type with the handle cast as an integral part of the vessel. This type is not exclusively Pennsylvanian in origin; however, many were made there. The rarest examples of this type were made in "Yorktown," Pennsylvania, by Elisha Kirk, who is also known as a clockmaker. The shape of Kirk's handles varies a bit from those made in Chester County, Pennsylvania.

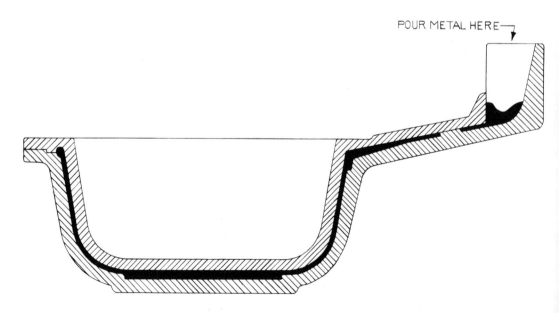

POUR METAL HERE

Top: Half of an original mold, presumably for a Pennock porringer. *Courtesy Henry Francis du Pont Winterthur Museum.* *Center:* Porringer probably made by Kirk, but lacking his touchmark. *Kauffman collection. Bottom:* Reproduction of top half of porringer mold and porringer attributed to Pennock. *Kauffman collection*

handle. Later, the top surface of the handle and the openings were made smooth; the bottom surface usually is rough, just as it came from the mold.

The second kind of porringer made of pewter is generally called the "solid-handled" type, and vessels of this variety were made in at least three locations. The most frequently advanced theory concerning some of them is that they were made for students, who used them for breakfast dishes at the Westtown school near West Chester, Pennsylvania. This supposition rests on uncertain ground, for when the writer visited the school many years ago, not only were there no such porringers in sight, but there was also no knowledge of the hypothesis. There were, however, a sizeable number of pewter bowls on a plate rail in a small dining room, which were reputedly used for the purpose assigned to the porringers.

These porringers consistently appear in Chester County, Pennsylvania, and were reputedly made by a Quaker named Pennock. About twenty years ago, the writer found half a mold, used for making such porringers, in the attic of a Quaker family living in southern Lancaster County, Pennsylvania.

Since that time, at least one example has turned up with the initials "S. P." imprinted on the handle, which may, or may not, indicate Pennock as the maker. The letters could also be the initials of the original owner.

Disregarding these hypotheses, it is probable that a bowl-basin type of porringer was made in Chester County, Pennsylvania, in the eighteenth century, and a mold in which this type was made does exist.

Curiously, a similar type of porringer was made in Yorktown (York), Pennsylvania, by one Elisha Kirk. Although the contour of the handle differs slightly from those made in Chester County, the greatest variance lies in the fact that most of Kirk's products have an intaglio stamp on the top of the handle with the imprint "Elisha Kirk, Yorktown." Little is known about Kirk; since a few clocks with his name painted on the face exist, one must conclude that he was also a clockmaker. Unfortunately, the only clock bearing his name seen by the writer was of a

Handle designs of round-bowled porringers ranging in size from 5½ to 2½ inches in diameter. The second from the left was made by Samuel Hamlin. *Kauffman collection*

very common quality; the workmanship very inferior when compared with the fine quality of his porringers.

Another solid-handle type with a handle contour distinctly different from those of the two previously mentioned was made by David Melville, of Newport, Rhode Island. On at least one of his examples his name is imprinted on the top surface of the handle. Thomas Danforth III, of Philadelphia, is also known to have made one porringer similar to the Melville product. His was marked on the inside of the bowl, a most unusual procedure for marking a porringer.

The reason for focusing attention on the two principal styles of porringers is the differences in making them. The hypothetical procedures for making the type with a bulbous body have been discussed as far as logic and knowledge permit; fortunately, there are no technological gaps in the making of the one-piece, bowl-basin, solid-handle type.

Very early and attractive porringer with a pierced handle resembling the style used in the handle of silver porringers. The maker is unidentified, but thought to have been an American. *Kauffman collection*

A complete two-part mold exists, each half being owned by a different museum, and porringers have been cast in the mold. The usual procedure of covering the inner surface of the mold to prevent pewter from sticking to it was followed, the mold was heated, and the molten metal was poured into the cavity provided for it. After the two parts were separated, the casting was turned on a lathe, the surface was burnished and finally polished with rottenstone.

American porringers of pewter are more plentiful than English ones and the solid-handle style seems to be one of the unique products of American pewterers.

CANDLESTICKS

An examination of references regarding objects of historic importance shows that although the subject of candle-making is extensively explained for the earliest times, the data about the evolution and styles of candlesticks is very fragmentary. Because of the importance of candleholders, particularly in the church, some specimens have survived and show evidence of the wide range and style that were made and used. Candles and candleholders were also very important in the home, but possibly because of their humble nature fewer of this type seem to have survived.

References support the hypothesis that some of the earliest examples were made of wood. The inflammability of wood caused the part which held the candle to be soon made of metal, and, finally, most of them were made entirely of metal or glass or fired clay.

The suitability of silver and pewter for making candlesticks might lead one to believe that many specimens were made of these metals. Their resistance to corrosion under normal circumstances should have caused many to survive; however, it must be regretably reported that neither is very plentiful today. A candlestick made of pewter, which can be positively identified as the product of an American pewterer of the eighteenth century is a rarity. As a matter of fact, neither the word "candle" nor "candlestick" appears in the index of the "bible" of American pewter, *Pewter in America* by Ledlie Laughlin.

The writer has taken advantage of the progress made through increased research and interest since 1940 (when *Pewter in America* was

published), to report the current status of information about some existing examples in America.

Fortunately, researchers, merchants, and collectors interested in objects made of pewter have been busy, and some very interesting examples have come to light. The most exciting finds have been two pairs now in the collection at the Henry Francis du Pont Winterthur Museum. These sticks are unusually tall, and fashioned in the style of European Baroque, a style frequently associated with objects of an ecclesiastical nature. A considerable amount of symbolism is found on the surface of these candlesticks, the most evident being the letters "I H S," which were originally derived from the Greek word for Jesus. Three letters were used, thus the contraction became "I E S." The similarity of the Greek "E" to the Latin "H" caused the change to "I H S." These letters have some legendary implications and are used by both Catholics and Protestants on objects connected with the rituals of the church. The surface of the candleholders have other symbols and decorative motifs, but most importantly to the student of historic pewter are the initials "I C H," for Johann Christopher Heyne, and the place they were made, "Lancaster" (Pennsylvania).

The technology of making these most important candleholders cannot be authoritatively discussed because they were not examined from that point of view. The likely procedure was to cast the various parts of sheet pewter and then assemble them in the traditional style of the period. It is particularly interesting to note that the earlier pricket used for holding candles was discarded by Heyne, and that he utilized the later socket which was widely used in America in the eighteenth century.

The gap between the two candlesticks discussed in this survey is not only broad in years but also in style. The small sticks of britannia metal of the nineteenth century are included because they were made in the

The constant mention of Heyne's name suggests that his products, particularly his candlesticks, are among the most desirable to own. One of a pair of candlesticks, 22 inches tall, is shown here. This has three flattened ball feet, three-part scrolled base, and the lower central shaft repeating the form of the base in miniature. The large upper bulbous shaft has a large circular drip pan. *Insert:* Each stick is marked "I C H" in a shaped shield below "LANCASTER" within an oval medallion on one side of the base. The two other medallions contain large engraved letters "I H S" surmounted by a cross. On each side of the central section is a cross and above, in a plaque, the letters "IN/RI." These letters stand for "Jesus Nazareth King of the Jews." *Courtesy Henry Francis du Pont Winterthur Museum*

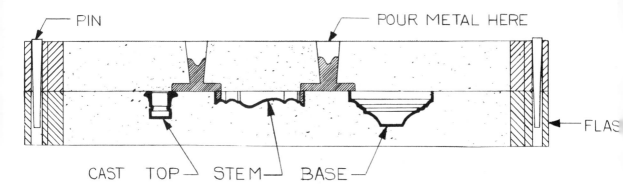

SECTION

Top: This sectional drawing shows how candlesticks such as those illustrated below were fabricated. This method of making the three parts separately to be assembled later was developed in the eighteenth century but lasted into the nineteenth. *Below:* Candlesticks, 6½ inches tall, were. made by the Taunton Britannia Manufacturing Company, Taunton, Massachusetts. *Kauffman collection*

This lamp made by the Taunton Britannia Manufacturing Company was fabricated in the same manner as their candlesticks. 7½ inches tall. *Kauffman collection*

traditional technique of the eighteenth century, and because their style appears to be earlier than the period in which they were made.

It is evident from the illustration that patterns for each part had to be made of wood, and later placed in plaster or sand for making duplicates of the wooden patterns. It is possible that more than one casting could have been made in plaster; however, if sand was used a new batch had to be "rammed" into the flask for each casting. Because the wall thickness of each part was so thin, the dampened sand might have been allowed to become slightly "dry" before a casting was poured. All of the parts are hollow for reasons of convenience in making, and for frugality in the use of metal. After the castings became hard they were removed, separated, and the worst irregularities removed with a file. The two halves of the stem were joined, and finally the top and bottoms were soldered to the stem. The final finishing and polishing was done on a lathe.

It seems logical to conclude that pewter sticks were made in the nineteenth century by a similar method, but the coming of fluid lamps caused some candlestick holders to be fitted with a "peg-lamp" of glass, or the metal was returned to the melting pot to be converted into an object of the latest fashion.

The alternate use of the stem on candlesticks and a lamp is a most unusual procedure, and foreshadows the arrival of the industrial revolution when such procedures were followed many times. The candlesticks and the lamp were made by the Taunton Britannia Manufacturing Company, the initials "T.B.M.Co." being stamped on the bottom of the stem.

OTHER OBJECTS

Bottles

The subject of bottles is of considerable interest to the collector of pewter objects, for at least two very interesting types were made of the metal. Possibly the most interesting, and certainly the most costly, are the dram bottles.

They are reasonably small, ranging from $4\frac{1}{2}$ to $5\frac{1}{2}$ inches in diameter. As a matter of fact, their name was derived because a small drink of spirits was often described as a "dram"—hence, "dram bottle."

The body of the bottles was cast in two separate identical parts, usually round and shallow, which were joined to create a form known today as a "pocket flask." A spout with a threaded metal cork was attached to the round vessel to permit easy filling or removal of the contents. The softness of the metal caused the fit to become loose (and probably leak); however, no gasket or other liquid retaining device has been found on one.

These items have always been held in high regard by collectors, and they virtually have a "halo" today. Most of the marked ones were made by Johann Christopher Heyne, of Lancaster, Pennsylvania, who reputedly made them for soldiers in the American Revolution. Spirits seem to have been a regular and important part of their rations. Heyne's products have his name stamped on the top or the bottom; however, the original cork has frequently been lost and identification becomes a matter of attribution rather than a fact. In this case, attribution seems to be less of a gamble than in some other cases, for lines and grooves were cut into the sides of his vessels and appear on most of them. An original cork can sometimes be detected by the teeth marks used to remove the cork when additional warmth was needed by a soldier.

Top left: Nursing bottle. *Top right:* Dram bottle. *Kauffman collection. Bottom:* Mold in making half a dram bottle, with casting in place.

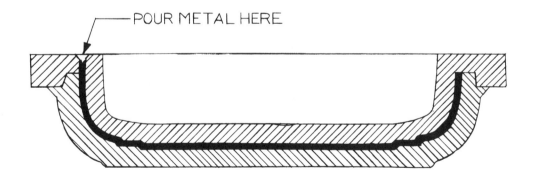

POUR METAL HERE

SECTION

Sugar bowl with lid and graceful knob. 5½ inches high. *Kauffman collection*

Of less importance, but of almost equal rarity, are the so-called nursing bottles of pewter. All examined by the writer were made by the casting technique of the eighteenth and early nineteenth centuries. They consist of three parts, a two-part body, with a horizontal joint at its greatest diameter, and a nipple, with an internal thread by which it is attached to the top of the bottle, through which the milk flowed. Most of them have dents, indicating they had been dropped on the floor or were otherwise treated roughly.

Sugar Bowls

A few sugar bowls can be found in collections throughout the country. Most of these charming objects closely resemble the form used by Baron Stiegel for the ones he made of glass; and curiously, most of the pewter sugar bowls were made in Pennsylvania where Stiegel was located. It might also be pointed out that both those of glass and of pewter were made about the same time. A few of the bowls retain their original lids. William Will and Johann Christopher Heyne are thought to have been the makers of most of the bowls. The writer has seen one with Heyne's name imprinted on the lid.

Chalices

Chalices by American makers of the eighteenth century must also be regarded as rarities. The most famous are by Heyne of Lancaster, Pennsylvania; however, some unusually handsome ones were made by Peter Young of Albany, New York.

The top and bottom parts were doubtless cast in one piece, while the stem was probably cast in halves, as other round hollow pieces were also cast. The two parts of the stem were joined lengthwise, after which the top and bottom parts were attached. The final finishing was probably done on a lathe.

Creamers

Although the three major components of a tea service were made in the eighteenth century, they were not made *en suite*. In the eyes of many connoisseurs, this procedure was an attractive one for an interesting variety resulted in the forms of the teapots, creamers, and sugar bowls. The most desirable form of creamer is really a miniature pitcher mounted on three cabriole legs with a "strap" handle. They are as rare as sugar bowls, perhaps even more rare. Most of the examples attributed to American makers are unsigned. However, one in the Laughlin collection was made and signed by Peter Young of Albany, New York.

Ladles

Although a sizeable number of ladles survive from the britannia period of the nineteenth century, many of which were cast in the tradition of the eighteenth century, examples of the earlier pewter period are very scarce. At least two examples by William Will, which were probably made late in the century, have survived. Both have typical round bowls with gracefully curved handles which are attached to the bowl by an overlapping end. This end is both decorative and very functional for it provides a firm mode of attaching the two parts. Both examples have

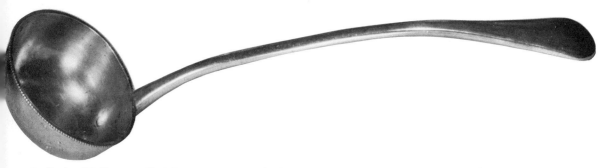

Ladle by William Will. This is just one of the outstanding examples of his work in pewter. *Courtesy John J. Evans, Jr.*

the exquisite touch of a Philadelphia craftsman—a beaded edge round the top of the bowl.

Salts

Open salts might be dismissed as unimportant products of American pewterers for extremely few, if any, bear the imprint of an American craftsman. They do, however, have the beautiful beaded edge of other Philadelphia products and it is very likely that a number of the examples extant were made there.

This chalice, made and signed by Heyne, is an outstanding example of craftsmanship in pewter. *Courtesy The Brooklyn Museum*

Pewter saltcellars of the eighteenth century are relatively scarce items today. They are obviously attractive and most of them seem to have been made in the Philadelphia area. *Kauffman collection*

It has been pointed out that funnels were formed both by casting and by fabrication from sheet metal. The joint in the neck of this one suggests it was made of sheet metal, probably in the nineteenth century. Some were made in the eighteenth century.
Courtesy Philadelphia Museum of Art

They were obviously cast in a four-piece mold and finished on a lathe. All the specimens known to the writer are round and could easily be finished by the rotary motion of a lathe.

Funnels

The *Oxford English Dictionary*, London, 1933, gives many definitions for a funnel, but the one of interest to collectors follows:

A cone-shaped vessel usually fitted at the apex with a short tube, by means of which a liquid, powder, etc., may be conducted through a small opening.

Funnels made of pewter can also be listed among the rarities; however, it must be admitted that they are not as eagerly sought as sugar bowls or chalices. European makers were more prolific in this category; and, although marked American examples exist, most of them are located in private collections or museums.

The ones made in the eighteenth century have no seams and appear to have been cast in a mold consisting of three parts. The inner core was the intended inner shape of the funnel, and the outer shell of the mold was made in two parts which could be separated after the funnel was cast. It is likely that funnels were also finished on a lathe.

One is known which has a shoulder at the upper end of the tube which rested on the neck of the bottle. Such an arrangement must have been very satisfactory, for the tapering tube did not then bind on the neck of the bottle, or possibly break the bottle.

Sundials and Clock Faces

Because pewter was made principally of tin, which deteriorated slowly when exposed to the weather, one might logically expect that an ingenious craftsman made some sundials of this metal. The scarcity of these objects can be easily explained by the fact that they had to be calculated for the latitude in which they were to be used, and obviously the high cost of molds prohibited the making of dials for many latitudes in America. At least one person circumvented the prohibitive cost of mold mak-

It is likely that sundials were made by a number of craftsmen. However, only one mold seems to have survived, along with a fairly small number of dials. They were obviously cast in a two-piece mold, but the flat portion is missing from the only surviving mold known to the writer. Mold of brass or bronze in which sundials were cast. The gnomon was cast as an integral part of the plate. *Courtesy Henry Francis du Pont Winterthur Museum*

Circular sundial made to be mounted horizontally; the latitude is not indicated. *Kauffman collection*

ing by engraving the lines on the dial, but this is a very rare example and most of them were cast. One example is dated 1762. However, a number of cast examples exist which are not dated, although some are signed by the maker, Joseph Miller, who probably worked in Connecticut.

An interesting excerpt about "Scientific Dyalling" can be found, with minute directions about the making of sundials, in *Mechanick Exercises; or the Doctrine of Handy Works* by Joseph Moxon, London, 1703, as follows:

> The Motion of the Sun is regular, it moving in equal Space in equal Time; But the Motion of the Shadow irregular, in all parts of the earth, unless under the two Poles, and that more or less according to the Constitution of the Sphere and Scituation of the Plane. And therefore Scientifick Dyallists by the Geometrick Considerations of Lines, have found out Rules, to mark out the irregular Motion of the Shadows in all Latitudes, and on all Planes, to Comply with the regular Motion of the Sun. And these Rules of adjusting the Motion of the Sun, may be called *Scientifick Dyalling*.

The time of the day (more or less) was determined by the shadow that a vertical triangle, called "gnomon," cast upon the various lines and numbers located on the surface of the dial. The cast sundials were made

Facing page: Unique sundial made of sheet pewter and engraved with the needed letters and numbers. This one was "Calculated for Lat. 40 Pensilvania"; also marked "Bedford April 7, 1763," Bedford, Pennsylvania, being the place of manufacture. *Courtesy Philadelphia Museum of Art; photo by A. J. Wyatt, staff photographer*

in a two-part mold, the gnomon and flat plane being simultaneously cast in one solid piece of metal.

Most sundials are cast of brass and the proper lines and numbers engraved on the top surface.

Pewter was also used on clock faces both for spandrels and number rings. These parts were usually mounted on sheets of iron which may have been painted or left to oxidize to create a color contrast with the parts of pewter. Presumably, the parts of pewter were polished occasionally, so a very pleasing contrast was created between the soft glow of the pewter and the darker metal on which it was mounted.

The spandrels were probably cast in plaster and the numbers on the ring were engraved; the tool marks being evident under the black paint which was applied so the numbers could be more easily seen. At least one other clock maker, in addition to Rose, is known to have made similar faces, and it is likely that many craftsmen followed this attractive procedure.

Clock faces were made of a variety of metals. The maker of this one must have been a lover of pewter for the contrast of the white metal with the dark background is unusually attractive. *Courtesy Country Inn Antiques*

Britannia

THE METAL

Hindsight has always been more precise than foresight, and thus from today's vantage point for observation it is difficult to understand why the inadequacies of old pewter were tolerated for so long by both craftsmen and customers. Of course, it is evident that an alloy containing a sizeable quantity of lead was superior to wood for the fabricating of vessels for eating and drinking. Pewter was certainly more expensive than wood for such objects, but for reasons of sanitation and beauty, alloys containing varying amounts of lead were used for centuries. The first pewterers' guild was organized in London in the fourteenth century, but it was not until the late eighteenth century that a better grade of alloy was widely used in England. This metal was known by various names, such as "Hard Metal," "Prince's Metal," "White Metal," and "Britannia Metal," and finally, only as "britannia," the word "metal" being taken for granted by all who were concerned with it.

In 1834, the new English metal was described by Dionysius Lardner in his *Cabinet Cyclopedia,* as follows:

> The composition of Britannia metal is as follows: 3½ cwt. of best block tin; 28 lbs. of martial regulus of antimony; 8 lbs. of copper; and 8 lbs. of brass. The amalgamation of these metals is effected by melting the tin, and raising it just to red heat in a stout cast-iron pot or trough, and then pour-

A workshop of the early nineteenth century. Much of the old remains, however. The wheel that ran the lathe was obviously large and powerful; the furnace was fitted with a stovepipe; and the tool rack was filled with reasonably modern tools. *Photo from Kauffman collection*

ing into it, first the regulus, and afterward the copper and brass, from the crucibles in which they have been respectively melted, the caster meanwhile stirring the mass about during this operation in order that the mixture may be complete.

The fusion of the whole being completed, by the continued application of fire for a short time under the pot, the liquid metal is, in the next place, transferred therefrom by means of large iron ladles to casting-boxes, which are composed of cast iron, and give the metal poured into them the form of a slab 15 inches long, by 6 inches wide, and one inch thick (to be later rolled into sheets). It is likewise put into other molds, forming small ingots, for the convenience of being used in the casting of such articles as are not made out of sheet metal.

From this description one can ascertain that the new metal was fabricated into usable objects by casting methods similar to those used in earlier times. The obvious need for a harder metal from which to make spoons and plates resulted in the use of britannia for these utensils, and later it almost completely replaced the older tin-based metal which contained varying amounts of lead. The popularity of britannia was accelerated by the invention in 1734 of another new metal, namely Sheffield plate, in which a base of copper was coated with a thin layer of silver. This metal was less costly than silver and brought many articles within the price range of the middle class, who were unable to afford objects of precious metals. However, it never became competitive pricewise with britannia.

Britannia metal had many inherent qualities which accrued to its advantage in the fabrication of metalware. Unlike other metals that had to be annealed for the rolling into sheets, britannia did not work-harden, and therefore could be rolled without any interruption in the process.

The soft, clean surface of the metal never deposited unwanted debris on the rollers which were highly polished—and had to remain so to function satisfactorily. Much attention was given to the exact thickness of the metal, a very important quality in subsequent operations, such as stamping and spinning.

Britannia had a number of qualities which made it superior to old pewter for the fabrication of objects. When polished, its brilliance compared favorably with that of silver, and thus it was known as the "poor man's silver." The longevity of its brilliance was also an attractive feature to the middle-class buyers, for they did not have servants to keep objects made of silver in acceptable condition.

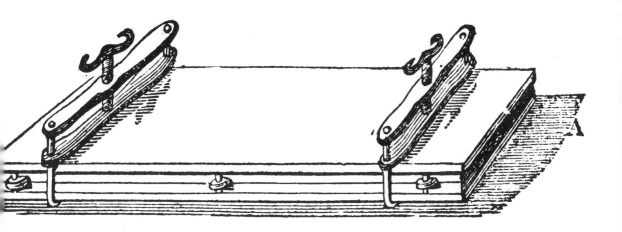

Casting box of cast iron into which molten metal was poured to form a small pig which
was later rolled into a sheet. From *Cabinet Cyclopedia*

Although the physical appearance of the metal was probably its greatest asset, it became competitive with silver and Sheffield plate because it
was cheaper and it could be fabricated easily (in comparison with the
other two metals) into useful objects. Lardner's description of britannia
focuses attention on the fact that it was cast in molds. The delay in the
transition from casting to other modes of production was probably
caused by problems encountered in rolling the metal into sheets. Until
rollers were made specifically to roll britannia some problems could be
expected. Until this primary problem was resolved, the major change
was in the improvement of the metal, and no revolutionary change was
made in the mode of fabricating it.

In 1834 Lardner refers to the early fabrication of the metal in England as follows:

> The principal if not, indeed, the only seat of manufacture of this metal
> is in Sheffield, where its composition and application on a large scale was
> begun about the year 1770, by two men of the names of Jessop and Han-
> cock. Its conversion into a great variety of beautiful wares gives employ-
> ment to about 500 individuals in that place.

The competition of English goods on the American market had always been a problem confronting craftsmen working here, and in this
field there was no exception to the rule. The highly-polished imports

with new forms and more lasting luster forced American craftsmen to make comparable objects of similar metal. The lack of scientific metallurgical expertise in this country probably caused many false starts before the new alloy was correctly analyzed and brought into production here.

One of the earliest accounts concerning the use of britannia in America is in the diary of Reverend William Bentley of Salem, Massachusetts. He reported that several men were engaged in producing such objects in 1814, among them being a Mr. Traske, who was trained as a silversmith and engraved some of his products to give them a distinctive appearance and a prestige which other plain products did not possess.

Perhaps the real beginning of the industry occurred in Isaac Babbitt's jewelry store, located in Merchant's Row in Taunton, Massachusetts. It is reported in *The Whitesmiths of Taunton* by George Gibbs that, when not serving customers, Babbitt turned out small articles of pewter on a foot lathe in the rear of his store. Early in the second decade of the nineteenth century he found that more and more customers were asking for the objects of britannia, then being imported from England. About that time Babbitt met William Porter, who shared his enthusiasm for discovering the secrets of the new metal, and, after many experiments with antimony, copper, tin, and zinc, their efforts were crowned with success in 1824.

About that time a William Crossman returned to Taunton from Castleton, Vermont. Babbitt and Crossman combined their resources; in a short time a plant was humming on the Mill River in Taunton. The riddle of the alloy had been solved. These men were joined by Ashbil Griswold of Meriden, and T. D. Boardman of Hartford, Connecticut. Soon there were factories producing britannia ware in other cities on the Eastern Seaboard and as far west as Cincinnati, Ohio, where Sellew and Company flourished from 1830 until 1860.

THE FACTORY

The existence of a small workshop with a master craftsman and a few apprentices, each of whom was trained to produce a complete product, was doomed for a number of reasons. Improved modes of transportation brought more mobility to the securing of raw materials and to the marketing of more products. The increase of population, particularly in remote regions of the country, created demands that could not be met *in loco*. Objects made in New England were transported by river vessels to port cities (for instance, from Hartford to New Haven), from where they were shipped to other cities along the Eastern Seaboard. There, merchants bought them for retail trade, or a peddler put them on his cart and set out for the hinterland. The shiny britannia objects were sold or swapped for items of value which were in short supply in the cities. One peddler reportedly returned with a load of feathers, which he easily disposed of, thereby making a double killing with his mode of merchandising.

Like most industrial movements, the transition from the small workshop to the large factory was slow. Men who had spent seven years as apprentices were loathe to have their knowledge and skills picked up by any "Tom, Dick, or Harry" in a few weeks or months. The old timers fought vigorously to perpetuate the accustomed ways of production. Entrepreneurs realized that the old methods had become inadequate to meet the demand, and soon learned that by teaching a man only one part of a trade, a specialist was created who quickly became competent in making spouts or handles, for instance, while others learned to make bodies or lids for teapots. By combining the skills of these men, a complete article could be produced in less time than when each man made an entire object. The Slater textile mill in Rhode Island was a major innovator in this new type of specialization, with its machinery being moved by water power rather than by old hand or foot devices. Throughout the first half of the nineteenth century both old and new types of production were in operation, but, finally, the small workshop dwindled in importance and the factory became a firmly established institution on the industrial scene of America. More modern methods were used to fabricate objects of the new metal. As a result, the market place was flooded with duplicates, well-made, but lacking the charm of their rare and alluring antecedents.

A number of integrated factors were involved in the creation and success of the factory: the improvement in raw materials, new designs, new machinery, and better sources of power. A subsidiary element, but nevertheless an important one, was the growing wealth of the country, which provided large sums of money to create industries employing hundreds of workers. This matter does not fall within the province of the present survey, and will receive little comment.

The subjects of metals has been previously discussed *per se*. In brief, the new trend arose principally from the fact that an improved metal became available; it was tough, it permitted easier and faster modes of fabrication; and its luster made it more competitive with silver, Sheffield plate, and slowly rising sales of objects made of clay and glass. Without these assets, objects made of tin-based metal would not remain competitive as long as they did. And without new machinery, new designs, and new power sources, the superior qualities of the metal would have been to no avail.

So far, only slight consideration has been given to American involvement in the development of manufacturing objects of britannia. This is due to the fact that the metal was originated in Europe, and the technological advances in fabricating it preceded those in America. From this point on, however, attention will be focused on the production of objects in America.

In the discussion of the metal the point was made that, at first, its use did not create a major change in production procedures, for craftsmen merely poured new metal into old molds. It might again be noted that making such vessels was not completely a hand process, for a lathe was used not only to make most of the molds, but also to skim the surface of the castings before they were assembled. As a matter of fact, the lathe never ceased to be an important machine in the industry; later, when objects were spun, it became a more significant cog in production procedures. Spinning the new britannia metal was not, however, the first step away from old-fashioned casting methods.

It is logical that the first departure from old methods was to fabricate britannia by stamping, a process used for shaping other metals at the turn of the nineteenth century. It was inexpensive, it required no new power source (just the hands and foot of a man), and the procedure could be carried out by one man. To perform this operation two dies (heavy blocks of metal with the desired contour) were needed—one called a "male" die, the other a "female." A piece of sheet metal was placed on a fixed die permanently attached to a heavy metal plate on a press or a bench top. The other half of the die was raised and brought down upon the piece of sheet metal by gravity or by turning a screw. It

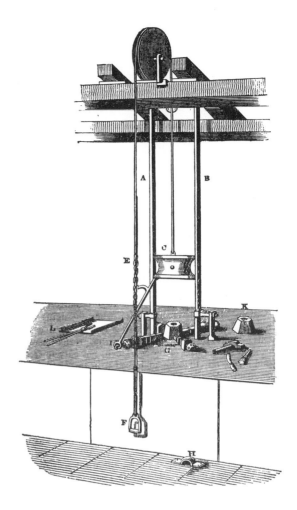

Stamping device operated by foot power for stamping out small objects of metal. Various dies and accessories are evident. The movable die was raised by pushing down with the foot in the stirrup evident under the bench. From *Cabinet Cyclopedia*

is reported that Babbitt and Crossman used a screw press to manufacture their first "teaware."

A press consisted of a heavy bed of metal with a large U-frame mounted upside down on its top; a large screw was mounted vertically in the center of the U-frame. On the top of the screw, a horizontal handle was mounted; and on the bottom, half of the die was attached and positioned exactly above the other half attached to the bottom plate. A portion of the vessel to be formed was placed on the bottom half and the top die brought down upon it by turning the screw. The momentum of the screw was sometimes increased by placing large heavy balls of metal on each end. Thus, by giving the handle a quick jerk the screw moved fast and positively against the metal to form it. The major improvement that this facility made to the trade was that the bodies of the objects no longer needed to be round, but could now be easily faceted, fluted, or beaded. Bodies of objects were made of a number of segments which were later soldered together, in combination with round bases or tops. The new technique created more versatility in style, with increased appeal and wider sales.

The use of a screw press had limitations, for in order to completely stamp a segment of a vessel, several "drops" had to be made, the first one only partially forming the desired shape, and subsequent ones finishing it. William Porter, the foreman of the Taunton factory of Babbitt and Crossman, constantly experimented with new methods, and in 1829 perfected a stamping machine which produced a complete part in one operation.

Two advances were made by Porter's new production procedure. The metal to be stamped was held tightly between two iron rings, which minimized the formation of wrinkles in the edge of the metal in a screw press, and the complete stamping could be done with one "drop" of the die. The new press was incorrectly called an "automatic" machine because the moving die had to be moved by hand only one way, up. The moving die was weighted and operated by a rope over a pulley. After the unformed metal was in place, the rope was released, allowing the die to fall with considerable impact on the sheet metal to give it the desired shape. The dies were made of brass, steel, or cast iron. The steel ones obviously were the most expensive, but also served for the greatest number of stampings.

The stamping process increased the variety in the design of the products and speeded up production somewhat, but continued pressure for more goods led ingenious men to turn to spinning metal, a technique that brought britannia to its greatest height of popularity in Europe and America.

Although spinning britannia slowly became famous in America (to Americans) it must be reported that, unfortunately, styles were for some time essentially English in character. The "high fashion" of drinking tea was gradually seeping down to the middle class, and most of the first spun items were connected with this custom. In 1829 the quantity of teapots made by Crossman, West, and Leonard (successors to

An invoice to Robert Coleman of Philadelphia from Canton, China, showing the items imported by him, including a sizeable amount of tea. The drinking of tea became a very fashionable pastime in the first half of the nineteenth century. *Kauffman collection*

Invoice of Merchandise shipping by James Latimer per & John Stocker Jr
on board the ship *Dorathea* M. D. Dougherty Master bound for Philadelphia.
for Account & Risk of Robert Coleman Esq a Citizen of the United
States of America & to him consigned viz.

R C 1 a 2 2 Boxes cont.g together & full One one Set of nankin			
		Blue Stone china	170
„ 3. 4 2 „ .		Ditto same a Priced	170
5 a 6 2 „ „		after Dinner Set Stone China 348/	161
7 a 8 2 „ „		Do same as priced	161
9 a 12 4 Boxes on 1 Tea Set china ea 126/	a $34		136
			$798
off 2/ per breakage			15.96 782 04

R C / H S 1 a 50 50 gr Chests Hyson Skin Tea N. 24 13 a 26 5 each 65			888 12
R C / J 1 a 10 10 Boxes best Imperial Tea	a $15.60		156 —
R C / H 1 a 10 10 Ditto „ Hyson „ „ 25 ea N.	. 19		190 —
R C / S 1 1 Box cont.g 25 ps Coloured Sinshaws	. 19		475 —
R C / J 2 11 ps Black Sinshaws on Box R C No 2 cont.g 25/f 18			198
			5100 16

          Charges
              Freight per Bill of Lading ———— $750
              Commission a 3/s ————— 153   903
                                                  Dr 6.003 16

Errors & omissions Excepted
Canton December 8. 1807.

                    Latimer a

              John Clements Stocker Junr

Babbitt and Crossman), was so great that their number exceeded the total output of all other vessels made by them. In addition to teapots, they produced coffeepots, coffee urns, lather boxes, tumblers, slop bowls, goblets, pitchers, and bowls. The factory system was truly emerging in Taunton. Schooners were sailing daily out of Taunton laden with local products, a large part of which was britannia ware.

The division of labor on Mill Creek in Taunton focuses attention on the fact that the factory mode of production had become successful and would continue to grow as resources and markets increased. In 1833 forty-one hands were employed, whose work was divided into categories such as machine and casting hands (a few parts continued to be cast), fitting and pressing hands, polishing hands, and finishing hands. Foot-manipulated "drop-presses" continued to be used, and wheels covered with moose hide or vertical layers of flannel cloth replaced the hand polishing of earlier days. Piece work became a common practice; and in 1833 four girls (!!!) were paid for washing and drying 847 castor frames.

Although the wheels were humming in Taunton in 1833, the same year the following report was published about Meriden, Connecticut, in *The Gazeteer of the United States.*

[Meriden] An important manufacturing place but with little water power: $1,000,000 annually produced: 1 company has 230 hands in making britannia coffee pots, spoons, coffee mills, waffle irons, signal lanthorns:

Crude power-operated buffer with a leather-covered wheel and a brush. This device seems very primitive by today's standards, but it was a great deal better than polishing by the famous "elbow grease." From *Cabinet Cyclopedia*

No. 1.—PRINCIPAL MANUFACTURES—Continued.

States and Territories.	Number of establishments.	BRITANNIA AND PLATED WARE.					
		Capital.	Cost of raw material.	Male hands.	Female hands.	Cost of labor.	Value of product.
Alabama							
Arkansas							
California							
Connecticut	25	$127,550	$201,399	406	90	$159,960	$441,050
Delaware							
District of Columbia							
Florida							
Georgia							
Illinois							
Indiana							
Iowa							
Kentucky							
Louisiana							
Maine	2	7,000	7,400	14		3,096	15,500
Maryland	2	8,600	5,500	16		6,036	15,000
Massachusetts	13	157,400	282,897	278	32	111,912	490,120
Michigan							
Mississippi							
Missouri	1	900	400	2		960	4,000
New Hampshire	1	2,000	2,000	2		960	5,000
New Jersey	8	165,400	143,947	115		30,756	227,765
New York	24	73,550	90,100	208	34	77,732	258,630
North Carolina	1	500	500	2		420	1,200
Ohio	1	500	500	2		960	1,700
Pennsylvania	9	46,700	25,516	69		18,984	71,400
Rhode Island							
South Carolina							
Tennessee	1	400	98	1		600	500
Texas							
Vermont	2	1,500	721	4		1,284	3,300
Virginia	1	150		1		480	600
Wisconsin							
Minnesota							
New Mexico							
Oregon							
Utah							
Total	91	592,150	760,978	1,120	156	414,140	1,535,765

Data reported in the United States Census for 1850, enumerating the number and geographical locations of producers of britannia and of plated ware at that time. There was a sizeable production at the time, and the total capital involved amounted to $592,150.00.

$200,000: other manufactures are wooden clocks [clocks with wooden works] value $50,000; ivory, boxwood, and horn combs value $40,000: auger bits and rakes value $20,000; tin ware value $90,000; another manufacturer of britannia ware $250,000; there are other manufactures of Japanned ware, shoes, boots; some very useful inventions have originated here; first branch of manufacture extensively engaged here was that of tin ware.

In 1883 the Meriden Bank was organized with a capital of $100,000, and opened for business at once or very shortly after in the old brick block on North Broad street still known as the "bank building."

It should be noted that, although similar modes of production were probably used earlier by other craftsmen in the industry, attention is focused on the factory at Taunton because of the report of events connected with it in *The Whitesmiths of Taunton*. In 1833, the aforementioned Porter made bearings of britannia, and the experiment was so successful that a patent was taken out on the innovation. In the following year (1834), however, Porter made the step which shook the industry, there and elsewhere, namely, the spinning of britannia. Despite the fact that this new technique was also patented, it was widely used by many craftsmen without any fees being paid or acknowledgment made to the man who had patented it. The final paragraph of the patent reads as follows:

> What I claim as my invention, and for which I ask a patent, is the forming of bodies of teapots, coffee pots, and other articles of Britannia or other metallic ware, or vessels from one piece of any metal capable of being so wrought, without the necessity of soldering seams, by taking flat pieces of metal, and giving them the required shape on the lathe, whether the same be done precisely in the manner herein described, or in any other dependent upon the same principle, and producing a similar effect.

Incidentally, about twenty years later a man named Hayden patented a similar process for the forming of brass kettles. It is obvious that patent procedures were not as definitive as they were purported to be.

A description of the spinning of metal should be prefaced with the statement that, although the process involved a circular motion, it was in no way connected with or similar to the spinning of thread on a spinning wheel. The earliest mechanism used in America probably utilized a lathe operated by water power. However, such a procedure apparently did not become universal until modern times, for a man who worked silver in the middle of the twentieth century told the writer he learned to spin the metal on a lathe with a foot treadle operated by himself. Buffers and other devices were probably also run by waterpower at Taunton from the very beginning of operation there. A turbine was installed by the Taunton Britannia Manufacturing Company in 1830; later a steam engine was installed for use when the water supply was inadequate to run the factory. Provision was made for each source of power to run the same machinery. In another point nearby, Ashbil Griswold powered his embryonic factory by an old blind horse traveling around a beam which communicated power to the floor above.

The spinning of metal was performed on a lathe. A chuck of wood with the desired shape was fastened to the headstock (the left end of the lathe), and a rotating tail block or follow block was attached to the tailstock (the right end of the lathe). A disc of metal was pinched tightly between the two mentioned parts by pressure applied by a screw fitting in the tailstock. A tool rest (not illustrated) was mounted on the outer edge of the lathe toward the operator, with vertical pins in it. The pins were used as a fulcrum for a long piece of wood or metal, one end being under the arm of the operator, the other end applying pressure against the surface of the lubricated disc as it rotated in the lathe. The speed of the lathe varied inversely to the diameter of the disc. As the disc rotated,

Typical lathe of the mid-nineteenth century. This could be used for turning wood or spinning metal. To spin metal, vertical pins of metal had to be inserted into the tool rest to act as a fulcrum for the spinning tool. The lathe could be operated by any type of power available.

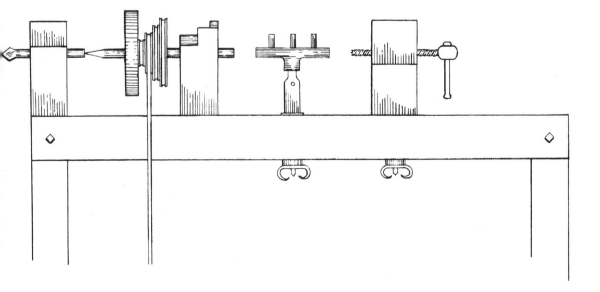

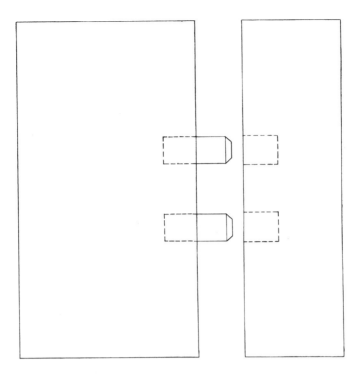

Step 1

To spin a teapot on the lathe on page 108, a two-part chuck had to be prepared with two dowel sticks inserted between them to keep them properly located in relation to each other, Step 1.

The two pieces were then placed in a lathe and cut to the desired shape as shown in Step 2.

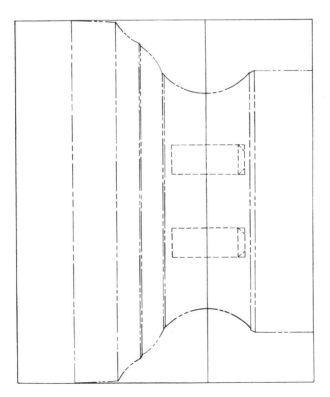

Step 2

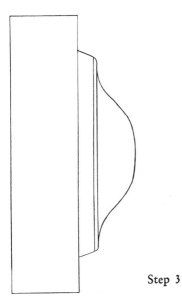

Step 3

A chuck was cut from a single piece of wood on which the lid was spun, Step 3.

The wood was turned exactly to half the shape desired for the teapot. The top and the bottom would be spun over this shape, Step 4.

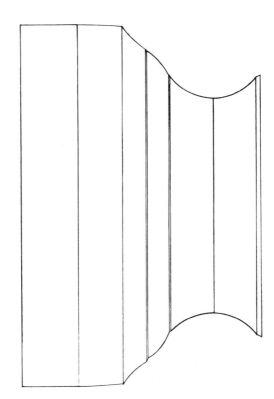

Step 4

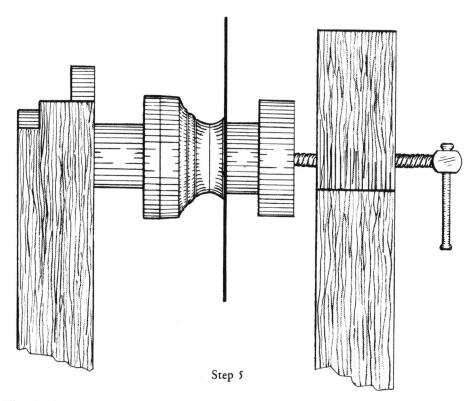

Step 5

The chuck was made smooth and a piece of metal the desired shape placed between it and a block of wood on the tailstock, called a "follow block." The entire assembly of three pieces rotated simultaneously. The disc was held in place by pressure applied by the tailstock screw. Step 5.

the spinner moved the end of the stick inward and outward until the disc fitted snugly against the previously formed chuck.

Thousands of duplicate parts, identical halves of teapots and other objects, were made by this method. The tops and bottoms of teapots were cut away on the lathe as a final spinning operation. A flat piece was inserted for a bottom. A lid was spun for the top, a process requiring little skill. The lid was attached to the top with a cast hinge, and the two halves were joined in the center by fusing small pieces of britannia metal into the joint in such a way that, under proper care and use, the seam could never be discerned on the outside of the vessel. It is usually very evident on the inside. One rarely notices a parting at the center seam; however, one of the pots illustrated does show a break. The spouts and handles were formed by the "slush" method used in the earlier era to form spouts for teapots and hollow handles for mugs and tankards.

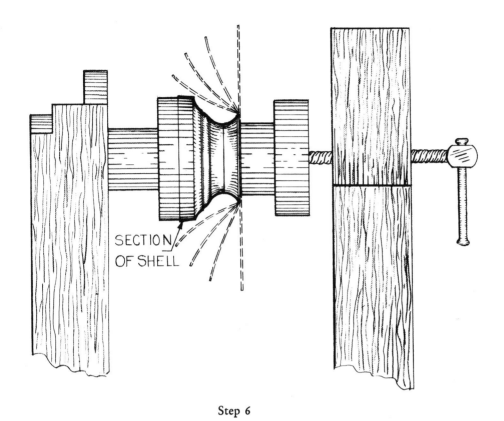

Step 6

As the spinning assembly rotated, pressure was applied to the disc and it was finally pressed to fit compactly against the form of the chuck, Step 6. A similar procedure was followed in spinning the lid, Step 7.

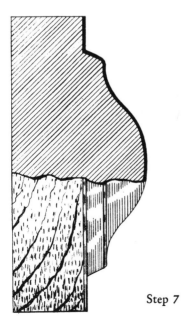

Step 7

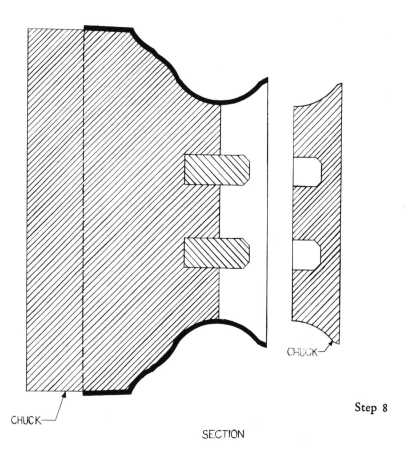

CHUCK

CHUCK

Step 8

SECTION

The bottom was then cut out of the spun form for half the body of the teapot, the small part of the chuck was removed, and the spun shell of the metal could then be removed from the larger part of the chuck. Step 8.

The handles of many spun pots were painted black to simulate the wooden handles used on earlier pots. Finally, the procedure turned full cycle; near the end of the era they were again made of wood, as they were in the eighteenth century. These, too, were painted black.

View of the various parts of the teapot before they were finally fitted and assembled. Step 9.

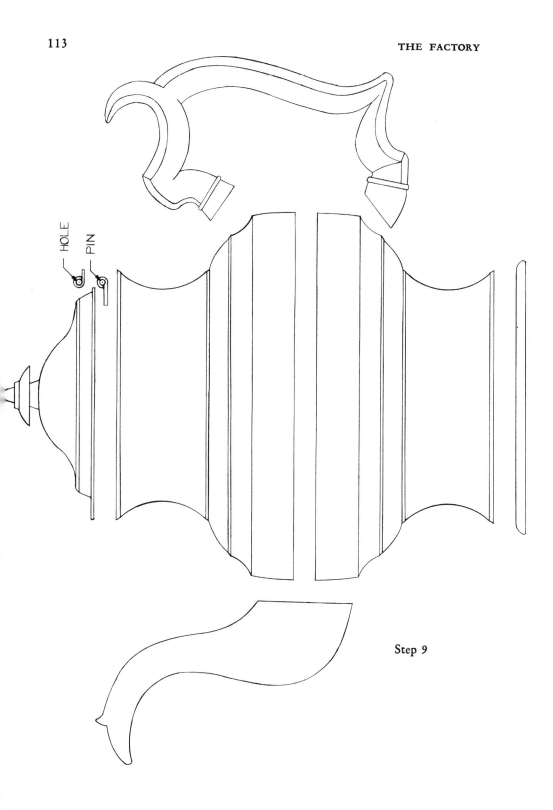

HOLE

PIN

Step 9

Although much emphasis has been placed on the making of a teapot, one should not conclude that they were the only product made of britannia. The tea urn was also a very popular item, as were castor holders, lamps, and candlesticks. Each manufacturer, also, probably had a specialty which he made to distinguish his merchandises from that of his competitors.

A final note about production of objects in the britannia era should call attention to a coffeepot, or teapot, commonly called a "light-house" type, which was not spun. These were either tall or short and had tapering bodies made of a cone of sheet metal. The joint extended from the top to the bottom, but was partially concealed by placing it under the spout or under the handle. It is usually evident because it was soldered, usually on the inside, and not fused with the metal of which the pot was made. The appendages were made as they were for the spun pots; some, however, were ornamented with beads "run-on" with a beading machine or swage designed to be used for the sheer-metal trade. The *pièces de résis-*

Three teapots spun in the manner described. The one on the left was made by Smith and Morey; the center one by the writer; and the one on the right is unmarked. *Kauffman collection*

Unmarked spun teapot showing a break in the center where the two parts were joined. The workmanship on these pots was usually very good and breaks of this kind are rarely found. *Kauffman collection*

Mode of adapting an older object to a new function. Many candlesticks were fitted with "peg-lamps" to use the newly found fuel, oil. *Kauffman collection*

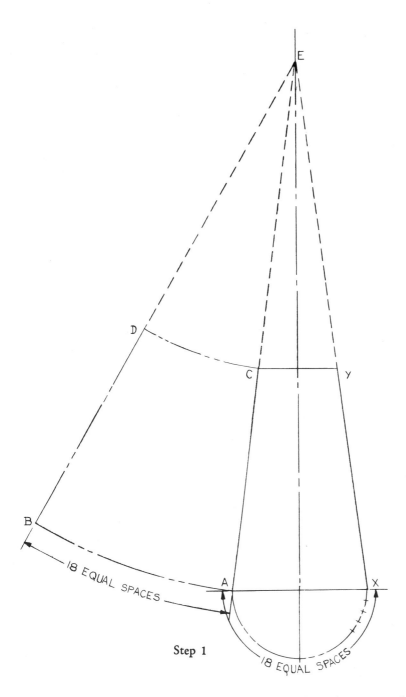

Step 1

In the making of a "lighthouse" coffeepot or teapot, the form C Y X A is the shape of the pot. D C A B is the developed form to be duplicated in metal from which the pot will be fabricated, Step 1.

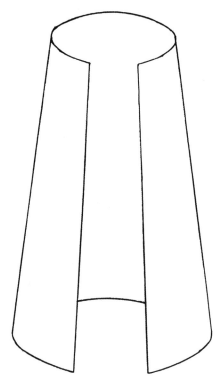

The tapering cylinder partially formed, Step 2.

Step 2

The form joined with solder, Step 3.

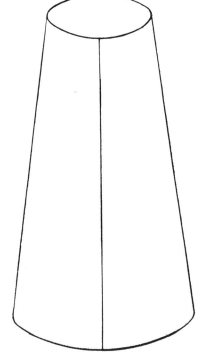

Step 3

Step 4

The various parts of the pot ready to be assembled. Step 4. Of course, a hinge had to
be inserted between the lid and the body.

Cylindrical communion flagon formed of sheet metal with the soldered joint being very evident on the inside. *Right:* In this case the joint is under the handle. *Courtesy Herbert Shiffer*

tance in this category are the ones made by Traske and engraved with restrained taste and great skill. Square shapes with rounded corners were also made in a similar manner (with a vertical joint); however, this style often rests on hollow balls of metal which dent the bottom after many years of use.

In 1845 the plating of objects made of sheet metal was begun in America and the death knell for the then old-fashioned britannia ware was sounded. Some companies, such as Sellew and Company in Cincinnati, Ohio, continued to produce britannia ware until 1860, but the freshness of bright, unplated, spun vessels had faded, the fashion of the fabulous 1830s and 1840s had had its day, only to be reincarnated by collectors in the 1950s and 1960s.

THE PRODUCT

Technology is usually defined as the practical application of scientific principles. Thus, when one examines the product of a new technological era, one naturally looks for evidence of change from the preceding one. For example, it is very evident to everyone today that the "space age" is different from the "horse and buggy era." In a less dramatic way the technology of the britannia period was different from the preceding pewter era, and the changes will be pointed out as they affected the nature of the objects produced.

It was mentioned in an earlier chapter that one of the ways britannia differed from pewter was that it was rolled into sheets before objects were fabricated from it, while vessels of pewter were formed by directly pouring molten metal into molds of brass or bronze. This new rolling

There were many variations of the spun teapot. A shape used by many was very similar to the one used by McQuilkin of Philadelphia. *Kauffman collection*

process was a very important one because it improved the surface of the metal, it made the metal tougher (as rolling usually does), it made it more uniform in thickness, and it provided a metal with more flexibility in the manufacturing process. The high cost of molds restricted the number to be made as well as the variety in any particular category, such as tankards or basins. In the britannia era these expensive molds were replaced by very inexpensive chucks of wood over which the sheets of metal could be quickly formed. The ease in forming and their low cost permitted them to be discarded without a great loss and replaced by a more fashionable shape or a variation of an older shape.

When viewing the range of objects made by the use of wooden chucks, one must conclude that the fullest advantage was not taken of the utility of the sheets in the manufacturing process. The reasons for this condition probably lies in the fact that the new mode of fabrication was embryonic, and its broadest use was not envisioned by the technologists of the time. It is also likely that when a saleable form was found, craftsmen were loathe to drop it for another with an unknown sales potential.

It must also be recognized that the use of these vessels was restricted to tableware, for the low melting point did not permit their use over a fire or on a stove. In the final stages of production a few enterprising manufacturers put copper bottoms on some of their products so they could be used on a stove. Of course, even these vessels could never be allowed to become dry on a stove or they would have been quickly destroyed.

Although these technological matters were of much importance in the new products, there were changes which were more evident to the prospective buyer. The new metal was whiter than the old pewter and, therefore, a more brilliant luster could be created on its surface. The brighter luster could also be attributed to the use of mechanized methods for polishing which replaced the older hand methods which were laborious and not as effective. In the nineteenth century the new luster was a definite asset; however, today's advanced collectors prefer the low luster of the metal with a lead content. One famous collector describes the low luster as "moon-glow." There seems to be little doubt that the leaded metal has a unique individuality, and an appeal not found in objects made of britannia, silver, or Sheffield plate.

A less evident asset of objects made of britannia was the fact that the

Two almost identical teapots by J. Danforth (*above*) and Savage and Graham (*right*), both of Middletown, Connecticut. There is some chance that both producers used the same equipment. *Kauffman collection*

American teapot in the Queen Anne Style (pear-shaped), but made in the nineteenth century. This pot obviously lacks the charm of the earlier pattern in the same style. The handle on this one is made of metal and was probably painted black when it was made. *Kauffman collection*

rolled metal provided a thinner medium for the fabrication of objects, and thus most of them were quite light in weight. This quality was not a particularly important asset except when a large vessel, such as a tea urn, was to be carried, or when large quantities of the ware were to be polished. It was obviously less tiring to polish twenty pieces of britannia than a comparable number of pieces of pewterware.

Finally, the most significant difference between the products of the pewter and britannia eras was their design. The older vessels were ob-

Communion flagon with a design derived from an earlier form, but executed and ornamented in the manner of the mid-nineteenth century. This example seems to be a fitting conclusion for the book for it was made by Ernst Kauffman in Philadelphia, Pennsylvania. *Mrs. Charles Kauffman collection*

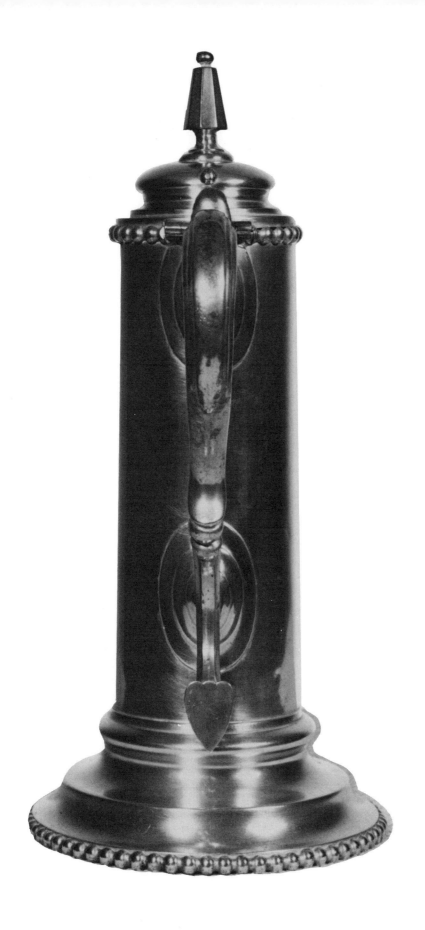

viously copies of earlier forms of silver; thus they had the rich classical forms which those of the precious metal possessed. The bottom portions of objects, such as teapots, had greater diameters than the middle or the tops, and moldings had the pleasing forms found on the architectural forms of ancient Greece. These forms were not only inherently pleasing, but were also compatible with the furnishings of the house, and the whole array made a setting which has really never been surpassed.

The most unfortunate aspect of much britannia ware, however, is the evidence of quickly manufactured parts that were assembled in several unfortunate ways. For example, the top and bottom halves of teapots were frequently the same, the two parts were joined in the center, and thus neither of the parts could alone be identified as a top or a bottom. An exaggerated statement might be made to the effect that the teapot was made of two bottoms or two tops. Such a situation was obviously not very disconcerting to the buyers of the period, but it seems rather obvious today that such a procedure was in the interest of manufacturers and not of discriminating buyers. It might also be pointed out that a few bowls have survived which are identical to half of a teapot. This procedure seems to be quite illogical and one would think that the shape of a bowl would not coincide exactly with one half of a teapot.

Although the aforementioned procedure was an unfortunate one, it might also be pointed out that a number of manufacturers produced objects which are amazingly similar in size and shape. Fortunately, some of these (coffeepots, for example) are more pleasing than many of the teapots, and thus the duplication of designs can be more easily tolerated in such cases. There was also great similarity in many of the lamps made by different makers, but occasionally a new and attractive shape came upon the scene. Most spun chalices were very similar; a number of manufacturers made large handsome pitchers, with or without lids. These items and some cuspidors, bedpans, shaving mugs, and a variety of spoons constitute the major output of the era.

The fast change of design and mechanical contrivances today focuses attention on the fast response of the population to new ideas and new products. Although, by esthetic standards, the older pewter was superior in design, the new metal with new fashions swept it away for a product which was superior in function, but certainly less attractive in its physical form.

THE METROPOLITAN MUSEUM OF ART

AMERICAN PEWTERERS

AND THEIR MARKS

NEW YORK, 1942

INTRODUCTION

The first edition of this catalogue was printed in response to innumerable requests for information about the pewterers who were represented in a special loan exhibition of American pewter held in the Museum from March 11 through April 16, 1939. Although this exhibition did not include the work of every known maker, it was the most comprehensive collection that had ever been assembled, comprising about 370 marked pieces, chosen for their form and variety and dating from the seventeenth, eighteenth, and nineteenth centuries. The marks of all but a few of the pewterers whose work was shown were reproduced in the catalogue; several were omitted as the owners' permission to reproduce them was not granted. The illustrations were made from photographs of plaster casts shown in the exhibition, several marks on one cast being from the same piece.

In reprinting the catalogue we have included valuable new information that has become available concerning American pewterers and their work. Most of the additions were taken from *Pewter in America, Its Makers and Their Marks*, by Ledlie Irwin Laughlin (Boston, 1940), a monumental two-volume book, the result of years of patient investigation that has revised much data heretofore considered definitive.

Pewter vessels have been in the service of man for many centuries, and they largely made up the tableware of our earliest colonists, who imported them from England and later made their own. Some of the seventeenth-century English importations, acclimated by long years in America, survive still, but no piece of native origin except a mutilated spoon recently found at Jamestown can be dated before 1700. Pewter continued to be the usual domestic ware until the lower cost of earthenware and porcelain in the nineteenth century weakened its popularity. There are other reasons why it lost ground for household use. An alloy made principally of tin, with small amounts of copper, antimony, and bismuth (and occasionally lead), the metal is not the enduring fabric that it seems. It disintegrates into powder when long exposed to damp and cold and soon melts when subjected to the direct heat of a stove. Furthermore, pewterware easily becomes misshapen and is often irremediably damaged by drastic cleaning.

The shapes in pewter are less versatile than those in silver of contemporary date, largely because the bronze molds which gave the utensils their form were too expensive to allow a wide variety. These molds were frequently passed down from father to son, and sometimes two or three generations of makers used them, with different marks to distinguish their work. The casting technique, moreover, did not lend itself to elaborate surfaces, but the well-balanced mass and graceful outline of many pieces are comparable to the best silversmiths' efforts.

JOSEPH DOWNS.

AMERICAN PEWTERERS
AND THEIR MARKS

Nathaniel Austin (1741-1816), Charlestown

Richard Austin (about 1773-1817), Boston

Thomas Badger, Jr. (1764-1826), Boston

Blakslee Barns (1781-1823), Berlin, Conn., and Philadelphia

Stephen Barns (working about 1792-1800),
Middletown (?), Conn.

Francis Bassett (1690-1758), New York,
or Francis Bassett II (1729-1800),
New York

Francis Bassett, Francis Bassett II, or Frederick Bassett

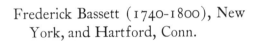

Frederick Bassett (1740-1800), New
York, and Hartford, Conn.

John Bassett (1696-1761), New York

Joseph Belcher (1729-1778), Newport, R. I., or
Joseph Belcher, Jr.

Joseph Belcher, Jr. (about 1751-after 1788),
Newport, R. I., and New London, Conn.

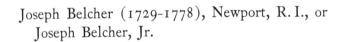

William Billings (about 1768-1813), Providence

Boardman & Co. (1824-1827), New York. Agents for Thomas Danforth Boardman and Sherman Boardman

Henry S. Boardman & F. D. Hall (1844-1854), Philadelphia. Agents for Thomas Danforth Boardman and Sherman Boardman

Thomas Danforth Boardman (1784-1873), Hartford, Conn.

Thomas Danforth Boardman & Sherman Boardman (about 1810-1854), Hartford, Conn.

Timothy Boardman & Co. (1822-1824), New York. Agents for Thomas Danforth Boardman and Sherman Boardman

Timothy Boardman & Lucius Hart (1828-1850), New York. Agents for Thomas Danforth Boardman and Sherman Boardman

Boston. Used by Richard Austin, Thomas Badger, Jr., David Cutler (1703-1772). Also used with the words Semper Eadem.

Parks Boyd (about 1771-1819), Philadelphia

Robert Boyle (working 1752-1758), New York

Cornelius Bradford (1729-1786), Philadelphia and New York

William Bradford, Jr. (?)
(1688-1759), New York

Timothy Brigden (1774-1819), Albany

Brook Farm (1841-1847), West Roxbury, Mass.,
probably used by Ephraim Capen (born 1813;
registered at Brook Farm 1844; working in New
York 1848-1854)

John Andrew Brunstrom (working 1783; died
1793), Philadelphia

Thomas Byles (?) (working 1738-1771), Philadelphia

William Calder (1792-1856), Providence

Samuel Campmell (early XIX century), Connecticut (?)

John Carnes (1698-1760), Boston

George Coldwell (working 1789; died 1811), New York

Oren Colton (working 1826-1836), Philadelphia. Sometime partner of J. B. Woodbury

Joseph Copeland (1649-1691), Chuckatuck, Nansemond County, Va.

Daniel Curtiss (working 1822; died 1872), Albany

Edward Danforth (1765-1830), Middletown and Hartford, Conn.

John Danforth (1741-1799), Norwich, Conn.

Joseph Danforth (1758-1788), Middletown, Conn.

Joseph Danforth and Thomas Danforth II

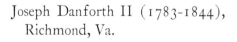

Joseph Danforth II (1783-1844), Richmond, Va.

Josiah Danforth (1803-1872), Middletown, Conn.

 Samuel Danforth (1772-1827), Norwich, Conn.

Samuel Danforth (1785-1816), Hartford, Conn.

 Thomas Danforth II (1731-1782), Middletown, Conn.

Thomas Danforth III (1756-1840), Rocky Hill, Conn., and Philadelphia

William Danforth (1769-1820), Middletown, Conn.

Benjamin Day (about 1706-1757), Newport, R. I.

Thomas Scovel Derby (about 1786-1852), Middletown, Conn.

Rufus Dunham (1815-about 1882), Westbrook and Portland, Maine

Simon Edgell (working 1713-1742),
Philadelphia

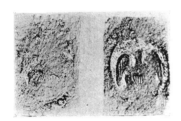

Jacob Eggleston (1773-1813), Middletown, Conn., and Fayetteville, N. C.

William J. Elsworth (1746-1816), New York

 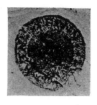

Gaius & Jason Fenn (1831-1843),
New York

Roswell Gleason (1799-1887),
Dorchester, Mass.

Samuel Green (1757-about 1834),
Boston

Ashbil Griswold (1784-1853), Meriden,
Conn.

Sylvester Griswold (working about 1820),
Baltimore

Hall & Cotton (working about 1840)

Samuel Hamlin (1746-1801), or Samuel Ely
  Hamlin

Samuel Ely Hamlin (1774-1864), Providence

Benjamin Harbeson (1763-1824) and Joseph
  Harbeson (1770-1822), Philadelphia

Christian & John Hera (working 1800-1812),
  Philadelphia

John Christian Hera (working 1758; died 1786) (?),
  Philadelphia

John Christopher Heyne (1715-1781), Lancaster, Pa.

John (?) Hill (working 1846-1848)

 J. & D. Hinsdale (working about 1810-1820), Middletown, Conn.

Homan & Co. (1847-1864), Cincinnati

 Henry Hopper (working 1842-1847), New York

Jehiel Johnson (about 1784-1833), Middletown, Conn., and Fayetteville, N. C. Sometime partner of William Nott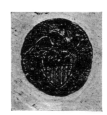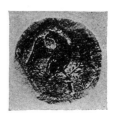

Gershom Jones (1751-1809),
Providence

Josiah Keene (about 1778-1868), Providence

Samuel Kilbourn (working 1794-1839), Baltimore, and Hartford, Conn.

Peter Kirby (working about 1736-1788), New York

William Kirby (about 1738-after 1810), New York

Elisha Kirk (working 1783; died 1790), York, Pa.

Moses Lafetra (working 1813-1817), New York

Joseph Leddel (before 1690-1753), or Joseph Leddel, Jr. (1718-1754), New York

Richard Lee (1747-1823), or Richard Lee, Jr. (1775-about 1858), New England

Lewis & Cowles (working 1834-1836), East Meriden, Conn.

George Lightner (about 1749-1815), Baltimore

William McQuilkin (working 1845-1853),
   Philadelphia

David Melville (1755-1793),
   Newport, R. I.

Thomas Melville (1779-1824), Newport, R. I.

Thomas and Samuel Melville (working 1793-
   1800), Newport, R. I.

William Nott (1789-after 1836), Middletown, Conn., and Fayetteville, N. C. Sometime partner of Jehiel Johnson

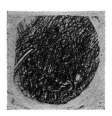

Ostrander and Norris (1848-1850), New York (?)

John Harrison Palethorp (working 1820-1845), Philadelphia

 John Harrison Palethorp and Robert Palethorp (working 1822-1825)

Robert Palethorp, Jr. (working 1817-1822), Philadelphia

 Samuel Pierce (1768-1840), Greenfield, Mass.

Plumley & Bidgood (working about 1825), Philadelphia

 Allen Porter (working 1830-1838), Westbrook, Maine

Freeman Porter (1808-after 1868), Westbrook, Maine

James Porter (working 1795-1805), Connecticut
   and Baltimore (?)

James Hervey Putnam (1803-1855), Malden,
      Mass.

George Richardson (1782-1848), Boston,
   Mass., Cranston and Providence, R. I.

Timothy Sage (working 1848), St. Louis

William Savage (working 1832-after 1860),
   Middletown, Conn.

Sellew & Co. (1832-1860), Cincinnati

Samuel Simpson (working 1835-1852), New
   York, and Yalesville, Conn.

John Skinner (1733-1813), Boston

Smith & Co. (1847-1849), Boston

 Eben Smith (1773-1849), Beverly, Mass.

Ebenezer Southmayd (1775-1831), Castleton, Vt.

  Spencer Stafford (1772-1844), Albany

Israel Trask (1786-1867), Beverly, Mass.

 Oliver Trask (1792-1847), Beverly, Mass.

Amos Treadway (1738-1814), Middletown,
Conn.

James Weekes (working 1822-1835),
New York and Poughkeepsie, N. Y.

E. Whitehouse (working early XIX century),
New York (?)

J. H. Whitlock (working 1836-1844), Troy,
N. Y. Probably an agent for Thomas Danforth Boardman and Sherman Boardman

Jacob Whitmore (1736-1825), Middletown,
Conn.

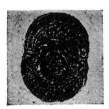

Henry Will (about 1735-after 1801), New York
and Albany

John Will (working 1752-about 1763),
New York

William Will (1742-1798), Philadelphia

J. Wolcott or J. W. Olcott (working about 1800),
Baltimore

J. B. Woodbury (working 1835-1838),
Philadelphia

Hiram Yale (1799-1831), Wallingford, Conn.

Peter Young (1749-1813), New York
and Albany

MARKS OF UNKNOWN PEWTERERS

I G (early XIX century)

Philadelphia

R. B. (working 1760-1780), Boston

Semper Eadem, sometimes with initials I S
(XVIII century), Boston

S. P. (late XVIII century), Westtown, Pa.

Spread eagle with stars (possibly Gershom Jones)

T. S. (late XVIII century)

Selected Readings

Century of Meriden, A. Meriden, Connecticut, Journal Publishing Company, no date.

Chambers, Ephraim, *Cyclopedia; or an Universal Dictionary of Arts and Sciences.* London, Printed for W. Innys, J. & P. Knapton, S. Birt, D. Browne, T. Longman, R. Hett, C. Hitch, L. Hawes, J. Hodges, J. Shuckburg, A. Millar, J. and J. Rivington, J. Ward, M. Senex, and the Executors of J. Darby, 1751–1752.

Dictionary of Machines, Mechanics, Engine-Works and Engineering. New York, Appleton, 1886.

Diderot, Denis, et al., *Encyclopedie, Dictionaire des Sciences, Recueil des Planches sur les Sciences, les Arts Libereaux, et les Arts Méchaniques.* Paris, Briasson et al., 1762–1777.

Gale, Edward J., *Pewter and the Amateur Collector.* New York, Scribner's, 1909.

Gibbs, George S., *The Whitesmiths of Taunton.* Cambridge, Massachusetts, Harvard University Press, 1943.

Kauffman, Henry J., *The Colonial Silversmith.* Camden, New Jersey, Thomas Nelson Inc., 1969.

Kerfoot, J. B., *American Pewter.* Boston, Houghton Mifflin, 1924.

Lardner, Rev. Dionysius, *The Cabinet Cyclopedia.* London, Longman, Rees, Orme, Brown, Green, Longman, and John Taylor, 1834.

Laughlin, Ledlie I., *Pewter in America.* Boston, Houghton Mifflin, 1940.
Appleton & Co., 1886.

Ure, Andrew, M. D., *A Dictionary of Arts, Manufactures, and Mines.* New York, D. Appleton & Co., 1886.

Verster, Ajg, *Old European Pewter.* London, Thames and Hudson, 1958.

Index

(Italics refer to pages of illustrations)

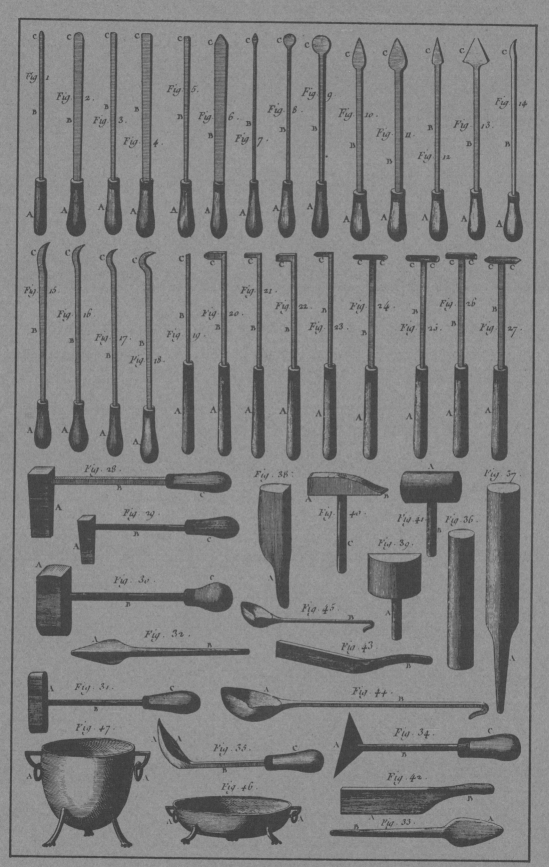

Potier d'Etain, outils.